# 92 Tips

## from the TRENCHES

ISBN: (paperback) 978-0-9904103-0-0
Library of Congress Control Number: 2014909297

www.92tipsfromthetrenches.com

Published by:
Delmar Publishing
Huntington Beach, CA 92648
760-900-0556
www.Ryder-Associates.com

Publicity rights: For information on publicity, author interviews, or subsidiary rights, contact Ryder and Associates: Tel: 760-900-0556 or email Marilou@Ryder-Associates.com

# 92 TIPS from the TRENCHES

## How to STAY IN THE GAME AS AN EDUCATIONAL LEADER

### Dr. Marilou Ryder
### Dr. Tamerin Capellino

DELMAR PUBLISHING
2014

*Also by Marilou Ryder*

*Rules of the Game: How to Win a Job in Educational Leadership*
Delmar Publishing, 2012

*The SeXX Factor: Breaking the Unwritten Codes That*
*Sabotage Personal and Professional Lives*
New Horizon Press, 2003

"Go to the Head of the Class"
*The School Administrator*, October 2009

"Superintendent Gets Taken for a Ride"
*The School Administrator*, February 2009

"Cultivating Women Leaders through a Network"
*The School Administrator*, November 2008

"Create Your Own Aspiring Administrators Symposium"
*Leadership Magazine*, 2006

"Moving on Up: Promoting At Risk Students"
*Leadership Magazine*, 2002

"The Impact of Male Gender Dissonance on Women's Potential
Eligibility forAdvancement to the Position of Superintendent"
*UNI Dissertation Services*, 1999

"Breaking the Statistical Norm: Women in Educational Leadership"
*Thrust for Educational Leadership*, 1994

# CONTENTS

*The foundation of my leadership style is to honor, validate, and show personal attention to every single person I deal with in all phases of leadership. A key to a long and successful career has been a mental toughness to overcome any obstacle and never relent, give up, or stop pursuing the goals and direction for myself, my team, or my organization.*

**Robert N. Griffith**
**Superintendent**

# Why You Should Read This Book

## *RECENT HEADLINES!*

### Teachers Vote No Confidence In Principal

Teachers at Ritter High voted "no confidence" in school Principal Robert Glass, several educators told district trustees Tuesday night. "There is a lack of communication on campus," said teacher Stan Smith. "Teachers, parents and students are not valued. ... He has failed our High School." Other teachers, who stood with "no confidence" signs during the board meeting, felt Glass has been unresponsive to their concerns, never praises anyone, and targets those who speak out.

### Superintendent Fired Over Vacation Days

Longtime Superintendent David Smith was fired this morning by the Richmond County Board of Education for not reporting his vacation days. "He's been taking days off from work and not reporting them," reported the board president.

### Principal Resigns After Allegations Of Affair With Security Guard And Drugs On Campus

An Arlington Middle School principal had an in-school affair with a security guard and failed to look into rumors that a cafeteria worker was selling marijuana to sixth graders, according to the results of an internal school system investigation. Bill Jones, who resigned as principal Thursday, said that the allegations are false.

### Middle School Principal Resigns After DUI Arrest

Star Middle School principal Rob Jones resigned earlier this month, just days after being arrested for driving under the influence. Jones, a 45-year-old Smithville resident, was arrested in the Star neighborhood, around 3:30 a.m. on Friday, May 7. The principal was observed by a motorist running a red light and crossing the median almost striking a pedestrian.

### Superintendent Resigns After Sending Sexy Emails

Former superintendent Joan Thomas, resigned earlier this week after it was discovered that she had sent some racy emails to someone from the district email account.

### Superintendent Fired For Credit Card Charges

While Richard Marks has been on administrative leave for the last two months, the board voted 5-1 last week to fire him. This decision followed an investigation, which found that Marks had charged about $800 in personal expenses to the district credit card, and did not reimburse the district for any of these charges. The superintendent said that he had been unaware that it was against district policy to make personal charges to the card, since previous administrators had been doing this for the past 10 years.

*Names and locations have been changed.*

According to current research, the annual turnover rate for school superintendents is between 14 and 16 percent. School principals, however, are another story. Of the principals who leave their jobs each year, the turnover rate is estimated at more than 40 percent, and about 10 percent quit voluntarily for a variety of reasons (Johnson, 2005). "Typically, the decision is made when the principal recognizes that problems exist that make the role untenable and that a change might be personally beneficial. The principal may be experiencing burnout, or realize that his or her idealized image of the role does not match the reality" (Johnson, 2005, p.21-22). The data about principals being fired varies according to what data is being collected, since many principals are forced to resign and asked to step back to the classroom.

To many, even educators in the field, the role of the educational leader has always been a little mysterious. Most people know that the superintendent or school principal is the ultimate "person in charge," but what these leaders actually *do* remains vague. The majority of educational leaders report that the role for them was a calling rather than a job. They believe they have an opportunity to impact and shape the lives of children that can change the future in profound ways. They know the job is difficult and are keenly aware of how vulnerable they are in the job but believe their "calling" and impact they have on society is compensation enough for all the hard work, stress, frustration and vulnerability they experience achieving their goals. They can't imagine having another career.

What does an educational leader really do all day? In truth, I sometimes wondered. As a principal, assistant superintendent, and then superintendent, it soon became clear that society had placed much on my plate and my power to influence stakeholders. State and federal mandates and special-interest groups placed a considerable burden on every decision I made and the time spent with parents and teachers demanding a seat at the decision-making table made me think I had little or no power to effect change. Working with board members, parents or students could take up the majority of a work day. More importantly, the standards-based accountability reform movement was built into my evaluation as a minimum expectation for the job. It was a tough and complicated job, but I loved every minute of it. It was thrilling to be able to impact students in such a positive way. I spent each day knowing my actions would make a profound difference on the lives of students and for me that was all it took for complete job satisfaction! I also knew that my actions, if not executed correctly, could cause problems for the organization, in addition to harming my professional reputation or career aspirations.

As the complexity of the job has increased, so have fears of a dwindling pool of qualified leaders. Research suggests there is an impending crisis in store for school leaders! Many quality educators are shying away from moving on and our nation's school districts are in desperate need of quality principals, district leaders and superintendents. Many leaders are promoted too soon to the position without adequate training, and they only last a year or two. Try it... type in the words, *fired school principal or school superintendent resigns* into your Google search bar. Don't be surprised when you find a new educational leader from somewhere in the country, resigning or being fired... every day! The job is difficult and takes an enormous amount of expertise, dedication, and leadership competency to succeed.

As soon as my last book, *Rules of the Game: How to Win a Job in Educational Leadership*, was published, I realized there was a more important story that needed to be shared. One day as I was presenting to a large group of educational leaders about key strategies to prepare them for securing a job in educational leadership, I caught myself telling the audience, It's *fairly easy to get the job... what I need to do next is write the book to help you keep your jobs!* The crowd laughed, nodding their heads in agreement. Soon after, I contacted a former school principal and convinced her to embark on the journey with me to write *92 Tips from the Trenches.* Our book launches from two key leadership roles; the school superintendent and principal. Topics covered include advising leaders to be visible, building relationships, becoming aware of social media, telling the truth, decision making and a host of other important areas. The book offers practical advice that many leaders can hopefully use to build their leadership skill set and stay at the top of their educational leadership game. In addition, throughout this book are many important quotes culled from leaders in the field to spark your thinking.

It's no secret that our country needs exceptional leaders to serve our schools and district leaders to provide organizational transformational leadership to remain globally competitive in a changing world. As co-authors we have both worked in the trenches, walked in your shoes and know that is fairly easy to trip up at the educational leadership line. And sometimes, it's the small things that you may not even be aware of or soft skills not taught in your administration courses that go unmentioned in leadership circles. We encourage you to take some time to flip through this important resource guide. Reflect upon a tip or two that perhaps you have not thought about or better yet, personally target a challenge area that could potentially harm your reputation as a leader.

There are thousands of books written to help people excel at their jobs once promoted. There are few books, if any, on the shelves today that focus on those aspects of leadership that can chip away at your career; that can cause you to lose your job or worse yet, lose your will to lead. This book aims to make your journey a little easier by offering some effective tools and "Insider Tips." Start reading, use what you can, and begin to reflect upon your own leadership competencies as you lead in your current position. If you successfully leverage some of these winning strategies, you will maximize your chances to make a difference for students and stay at the top of your leadership game. If you tear a page out to post on your wall, put a sticky note on a page or highlight any of the passages in this book, we've done our job. Consider this publication your personal score card to define and improve upon your educational leadership skills. While the journey may be long and hard, we can assure you there is nothing more rewarding than to serve as an educational leader to make a positive difference for students by leaving a lasting legacy. *Now let's get to work and make it happen!*

---

Johnson, Lori A. "Why Principals Quit: There Are Many Reasons Why Principals Voluntarily Leave The Positions They Worked So Hard To Earn." *Principal*, v84 n3 p21-23 Jan-Feb 2005

Sashway, Larry. "The Superintendent in an Age of Accountability." September 2002. *Eric Digest* 161.
https://scholarsbank.uoregon.edu/jspui/bitstream/1794/3387/1/digest161.pdf

# Introduction

*by Dr. Marilou Ryder*

My father, a businessman by trade, loved football and made it his life's mission to attend every Super Bowl in person. As a child, I recall how our family would spend each cold, blistery Thanksgiving holiday encouraging our father to join us at the dinner table. In spite of my mother's frustration, my father would jockey back and forth between the dining room and living room in an attempt to watch three separate football games. His games were viewed on three different televisions scattered around the living room. If alive today, I am confident he would own a television that would allow him to watch at least six games simultaneously on one screen.

He was a father of five children, all daughters, and couldn't revel in the pleasure of watching a son play football. I suspected this twist of fate for him was pure agony. Lacking sons to feed his football habit, he came up with his own bright idea to fill the void; he created a football team. He called this team the Syracuse Stormers. As a successful businessman he used his talents to encourage the other town fathers to support his plan. Gradually he persuaded them to fund a new city football franchise, and within a year the Stormers were off and running. They were an exciting new junior league football team and my father was now actively recruiting third-string players from the Buffalo Bills to fill the team roster. I was twelve years old at this time and very impressionable.

For the next five years our home was filled with football players, businessmen, trainers and coaches. Our garage was filled with helmets, jerseys, football sleds and shoulder pads. Steve

Owens, former All American football player and New York Giants head coach Hall of Famer, was recruited to coach the Stormers. Owens spent the next two years in our living room working with my father, always with a drink in one hand and a cigar in the other. He spoke with a rough gravelly voice, which scared me as a kid. I later learned this was the result of his fondness for chewing tobacco. Our house was no longer just a home… it was an exciting athletic training center. At the time, it seemed that everyone in town wanted to be part of the team in one form or another. I became the envy of every kid in school.

So what does this story have to do with leadership? Growing up as a young female surrounded by football fanatics provided me with some key learning experiences for both life and leading. Coach Owens' talent for coaching football and his strategies for scoring points and winning games fascinated me as a young girl. I soon learned that scoring points is the lifeblood of a sports team.

Since winning teams sell tickets, my father's biggest fear was focused on the irrefutable fact that if his Stormers didn't win, they may not last another year… if they didn't score points, they wouldn't sell enough tickets for the next game to pay the players. That's all anyone talked about… points. Who scored the most points? Who didn't score points? Who almost scored points but fumbled in the final seconds? How many points in the first quarter, the first half and then the overall game? Every day men could be found huddled in our living room rummaging through reams of paper, deliberating over the "points." And everyone in the room knew that Coach Owens and my father expected the very best from each and every player.

In every game, if a ball was fumbled or a pass not caught in time, my father would scowl and curse. When points were scored or the Stormers won a game, he would become the best father anyone could ever hope for… smiling, hugging his family and friends and celebrating by treating everyone, including the cigar smoking, point-scoring coach to dinner at the best restaurants in town. This scenario went on for two years.

Then one day my father surprised everyone when he stood up after dinner one night, and abruptly announced, "Just for your information, I'll be shutting down the franchise after next week's game." My mother must have been in on this news, since she didn't seem to show any reaction. I was overcome with shock and disappointment; I loved attending the games, was the envy of all my friends at school and would miss my quality time in the living room with the guys. I started to interrupt and shout out in protest, in concert with my older sister, until my father held up his hands and said, "Settle down now, let's just calm things down a little."

"We just didn't win enough games to go another year," my father went on to explain. "Not too many people know this, but Coach Owens has been working for free these last two games and we don't have enough money in the bank to pay the players; we can't finance another season." I felt really sorry for myself that day, but even sorrier for my father; he had a great football vision for our city but we all knew that the team didn't score enough winning "points" to attract an ongoing fan base. While the city was initially excited about a new sporting opportunity, their enthusiasm waned when they realized that the Stormers hadn't proved to be a winning team.

As the daughter of a football junkie, I was introduced to leadership early on. As I grew older, reading and learning about leadership was pure pleasure. I combed through study after study, absorbing as much as I could about leadership. I dreamed of the day when I would lead and take people places they dared not venture themselves. As a young educator, I had a vision for transforming schools to meet the needs of students and communities. And I was sure I had the knowledge to make that happen.

Shortly after becoming a school principal, I found myself recalling the days of the Syracuse Stormers... the team and Coach Owens inspired me to think about leadership in much the same way as a football game... *Points*. As a leader I knew it was important to acknowledge people's accomplishments and often found myself in situations that involved awarding "points" for good deeds. For example, during my first year as a middle school principal I caught myself, in mid-sentence, awarding my assistant principal "points" for solving a problem with a volatile parent. The assistant principal and I were both keenly aware that if he couldn't handle the issue, all hell would break loose and make its way to the superintendent. "Thanks for your due diligence in handling this problem," I said. "That's two extra points for you!" "Two points," my assistant principal probed, "what are the points for... is someone keeping score?" There it was, plain as day.... my own leadership philosophy had evolved... I was keeping score.

Leadership can be thought of as a game where you accumulate points. When goals are reached, or when we do the right thing as a leader, we get points. We enter these points on our personal leadership score card. In the field of leadership, as in sports, we can "fumble the ball." Essentially when leaders do things that aren't so great, like publicly scold an employee or write an inappropriate email, or wear an inappropriate outfit to work... they hand over control of the game to their followers, who in short order, lose confidence in them as leaders. The fine art of leadership, in my opinion, is obviously to score as many points as possible and not fumble the ball. Too many fumbles and followers not only lose confidence in their leader, but fumbles take leaders down and limit their potential to move organizations forward to new levels of excellence. Fumbles stop forward motion and turn over control to the very people you have been charged with leading. Points on your personal score card are extremely valuable if you want to play another season.

I have witnessed too many leaders with an abundance of points on their leadership score cards lose the game with just one or two callous behaviors or stupid mistakes. I have observed leaders with great potential use poor judgment by having too many alcoholic beverages in public and have those in attendance conjecture their leader had a drinking a problem. I've known leaders to lose their fan base overnight after an adulterous affair was made public. And I have worked with leaders leveraging school boards for personal pay raises in spite of dwindling instructional resources causing the rank and file to complain. More than once I heard them question the "real" reasons their leaders took the position in the first place. As a result, some of these leaders did not score enough winning points for another season... much like the Stormers.

Richard Carlson rose to fame in 1997 with the success of his book, *Don't Sweat the Small Stuff...and it's all Small Stuff*. He wrote one of the fastest-selling books of all time and changed the way many people approached life. I loved his theory; it made so much sense to me... at first. But over time, I learned that it's the accumulation of all the small stuff in life that can cause some big trouble, especially for leaders. I believe that leaders must give their full attention to the "small stuff," maybe not work up an actual sweat in the process, but stay tuned to the small things that can have a big impact on one's ability to earn leadership "points." It's a sign of impending failure if you arrive at the "tipping point" where keeping or losing your fan base is at stake. If you accumulate leadership points, if you continue to score goals rather than fumble for your organization, your fans may even be willing to purchase a season ticket.

*Good Leaders don't sweat the small stuff; great leaders sweat everything. Some educational leaders forget the small things like saying hello, knowing people's names, and being visible. Also, I have found personal notes and cards to school employees really go a long way. In my 32 years as a school and/or district administrator I have found my greatest professional successes occurred because my boss believed in me, and trusted me to do what is right for the children and for the organization. Now, as a superintendent, I find that our greatest organizational successes have occurred when we empower, believe in, and trust our employees to do the right things for our students.*

**Dr. Jonathan Greenberg**
**Superintendent**

# 92 TIPS FROM THE TRENCHES

*Over the years I have learned a lot about leadership and am convinced it is more art than science. Some characteristics I think are essential are having a vision to see into the horizon while still being grounded in reality; a genuine care for the people you work with; a relentless pursuit of strategic, team developed goals; and perhaps most important... perseverance - there will be many challenges and obstacles, but never give up driving towards improvement and evolution.*

**Dr. Andrew Shean**
**Vice Provost, Curriculum and Innovation**
**Ashford University**

# 1. FIRST ACCOUNT

Always assume the first account you receive of something serious many not always be accurate. Check it out thoroughly before you act.

I recall the day one of our students charged into my office, practically gasping for air to report that the new substitute teacher was allowing students to perform lap dances in the cafeteria.

Before I could even think *child molestation* I ran down to the cafeteria and saw that the cheer squad was practicing quite normally in full view of the substitute PE teacher. I noticed, however, that these new dance routines were being presented too close to the substitute's chair. I starting asking myself... why is this guy sitting down, and then began to speculate that my informant must have seen something inappropriate.

Without jumping to conclusions, I gestured to one of the known reliable cheerleaders to come and speak with me. I asked her in confidence if there was any truth to the boy's assertion and she assured me that everything was just fine and not to worry. My *informer,* she confided, had been sent to the principal's office by the substitute teacher for harassing the girls during practice. Nonetheless, I had a follow-up conference with the substitute teacher, reminding him that he needed to be on his feet and not sit in a chair when teaching physical education.

Remember, take informant information seriously and try to contain your emotions and not overreact. But, always follow up diligently to ensure that all is good...or maybe not.

## 2.  BUY THE GIRL SCOUT COOKIES

Y ou know the saying: if you plan to make a lot of money, expect to pay high taxes, right? Well, the same thing can be said for purchasing items from your students or clubs.

As a principal, assistant superintendent and superintendent, I made a respectable salary and knew it was important to allocate a certain percentage of my salary each year for Girl Scout cookies, athletic fund raisers, magazine sales and foundation events. In a leadership role you don't want to be known as the person turning down a student who is encouraging you to purchase a box of Girl Scout cookies. But we also can't fulfill every student's request and there's a limit to how much we can spend each year donating to good causes. Knowing that, I would subtly inform various clubs and students that I had a cookie dollar limit which did not include purchasing a million boxes, but if they approached me early I would buy their products. The good news was that students were fairly intuitive about this feature of fundraising and seemed to know the purchase limits of top leadership.

So the deal is this: if you know you can afford 20 boxes of cookies, or 10 cartons of cookie dough or $500 to the education foundation, plan on a reasonable amount in advance, and stash it away for contributions to student causes. When you approach fundraising in this manner, your money will be well spent. You don't want to get trapped in a situation where you turn down your kids. Also, since I was continually watching my weight, whenever I purchased edible items I would donate them to the staff lounge or offer them to my secretary.

Nobody wants to think of their leader as someone who's cheap, so it's important to know what percent of your salary you can comfortably allocate to make students and parents happy by acknowledging certain programs with your contributions. As a superintendent I donated a certain percent of my salary each year to our educational foundation. The amount was always recorded in the minutes and served as a model for employees, who were being encouraged by the Foundation to also donate. Reserve some cash in your pocket for programs you want to openly support as worthwhile for students. The advice is clear... *buy the Girl Scout Cookies.*

# 3. KEEP YOUR WORD

When you purchase a product that claims to brighten your laundry, clean your floors spotless, or ease your pain, you expect the product to follow through on their promise, right? What happens when you discover your whitening detergent is a hoax, your floors look okay but still have a dull residue on them or your head is still throbbing after taking that medication? You feel like you've been duped and will probably never buy that product again, right?

As an educational leader, what happens when you promise something and don't follow through? Same thing. People stop trusting you. The size of the promise makes no difference; if you promise that you will call someone at 4 p.m. and don't make the call until 4:15, you have not kept your word. And your word goes a long way in leadership. If you promise parents that you will look into the unsafe bus routes and do not follow through, people will learn not to believe you.

Often, when confronted with an angry constituent, leaders have the tendency to skirt the problem by promising people things they can't deliver. I've witnessed this scenario repeatedly throughout my career. Be careful with your word, it is worth more than you think. Keep your word and you will be respected, trusted, and admired throughout your entire leadership career.

# 4.  WINNERS CAN BE LOSERS

I f attending an event, purchase a few raffle tickets. However, if you win, that's another story. If you win, and don't play your cards right, you can lose big time.

If you publicly earn the big prize at a Chamber meeting, an employee event, or PTA type function, you can do one of two things; donate the raffle ticket back to the group by stating "Go ahead, pull another raffle ticket, I'm good" or in the case of a 50-50 raffle, offer the prize money back to the group selling the ticket. (However, all rules are off if you win a bottle of wine or centerpiece as the exiting door prize; feel free to ignore this tip altogether.)

I followed this *leadership tip* early in my career when attending an important CSEA Friday night dinner event. Dinner with these union folks was the last place I wanted to be at the end of a long week. I was exhausted, but I knew it was important for me to be seen professionally at their event. As soon as I walked in I was approached by the union VP to purchase some raffle tickets. I bought ten tickets and spent $40 for the sponsored 50-50 club. At the time I wasn't particularly in good favor with CSEA as I was making a lot of changes to the district as the new superintendent. They didn't like it one bit and shared their opposition openly.

My main reason for attending the dinner was to demonstrate that I cared about them and validated their accomplishments as an employee group. All throughout the dinner I felt that CSEA members were beginning to warm up to me somewhat, and I soon recognized my attendance was not in vein. The big payoff for the evening came when my ticket was pulled from the basket and the CSEA President announced that *the Superintendent* was the winner of the big prize. Cheers and respect came when I immedi-ately, now take note ... *immediately,* smiled at my winnings and donated the $340 back to CSEA. I soon became their Friday night hero, as most couldn't believe anyone would ever donate that amount of prize money back to the group. On Monday morning, the first thing people talked about was my good luck for win-ning the prize and CSEA's good luck for having such a *generous superintendent.*

# 5. LEADER OF THE PACK

P art of your leadership role as a school administrator, district office staff member or superintendent will undoubtedly involve attending numerous professional developments, school presentations and workshops. If you require your leadership team to participate in leadership training, it is important that you *put your money where your mouth is* and attend these sessions with them.

Nothing is more important than training leaders to be better at what they do. Your attendance at these events is critical to emphasize your belief in them and to support their growth as leaders. The same is true for teacher trainings. As a superintendent I always stopped in on these sessions to address the crowd and thank them for their dedication to continuous learning. I only stayed a short time, however, as a principal I made sure to attend teacher trainings in their entirety.

Given that we like to multitask and it's easy to run out of the staff development meetings because our presence is needed somewhere else, try really hard to avoid this habit. Make time to attend these sessions, participate in the training, and model what you preach. Also, at the conclusion of trainings, there are always a few people left holding the bag, having to clean up, move chairs, and collect up chart paper and supplies. Stick around and help them. Show those you lead that you are not beyond helping them with the final details. After all, you *are...* *THE LEADER OF THE PACK*.

*Three great quotes that I have used throughout my career include:*

*"Great leadership seems to be appreciated most when it is gone..."*

*"Leadership is not about you......it's about others."*

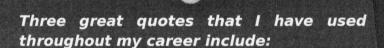

*"Some folks are always looking for greener grass. Water and fertilize where you are....then, you'll be in green grass."*

**Dr. Philip O. Pendley**
**Retired Superintendent**

## 6. CAUTION: RETREATS CAN BE HAZARDOUS TO ONE'S HEALTH

Although the practice of having offsite "retreats" is diminishing, some schools and districts still participate in yearly staff retreats. Retreats are meant to build cohesive teams, build organizational culture, boost morale, and focus on organizational goals, but they often can go awry. Some social events incorporated in staff retreats become legendary workplace folktales shared years later. Caution should be taken when mixing business with pleasure.

I was hired as a new principal in a school district where offsite administrative staff retreats were part of the culture. These *voluntary* events felt anything but *voluntary*. The first year, I packed my bags and reluctantly left my family for two nights to spend time with my new colleagues. Being new to the organization, I tried to maintain a low profile and spend time observing the dynamics while slowly building relationships with my new colleagues. It did not take long before I started hearing stories of past retreats... The time so and so, a first year principal, was drunk and bought shots for board members and rumors of "flings" between colleagues. By dinner, there were several colleagues already intoxicated and before long, the Assistant Superintendent was dancing on top of a chair. The room cheered and roared with laughter. It was clear to me this behavior was encouraged, which really discouraged me as a new member of the team.

Over the next few years, the mayhem intensified. Shortly thereafter, a lawsuit ensued against the district for sexual harassment, discrimination and hostile work environment. The "cost" of the retreats quickly became far more than just monetary. The district suffered bad press in the form of numerous news articles printed in papers and posted online across two counties. The story even hit nationwide educational blogs, where the district was blasted for frivolously spending taxpayer money. The series of stories not only hurt the credibility and profession-alism of district officials, but compromised the reputation of the entire administrative staff. It was a complete embarrassment. A dark cloud loomed over everyone's head, regardless of the level of involvement. So much for boosting morale! Careers were also damaged along the way. One assistant superintendent, selected for the top seat in another district, found himself in a bad posi-tion after the community and board members found out about the lawsuit and stories of "risqué behavior" at the retreats. The deal eventually fell through and he was not offered a contract in that new district.

If you are required to attend a staff retreat or conference, exhibit extreme caution before engaging in any lighthearted activities. If the retreat entails an overnight stay, bring your spouse or significant other if at all possible. Avoid socials such as *Happy Hours* or *Meet and Greets* that include alcohol. If you feel compelled to make an appearance, make it brief and drink water or soda, preferably out of a can so it is clear what you are drinking, or more importantly what you are NOT drinking. At the end of the day, retreat to your room or return home as quickly as possible after thanking your boss.

## 7.  DRESS FOR SUCCESS

E ntire books have been devoted to the subject of professional work attire. I wrote a chapter on the subject in my book for women gaining access to top leadership positions entitled, *The SeXX Factor: Breaking the Unwritten Codes that Sabotage Personal and Professional Lives.* I concluded that one should not dwell on this issue. Simply dress for the job.

Administrators, on their best days, wear suits and ties. As a leader you must send the right message and people should think that you are in charge. Even though the rules at work have changed a bit with a more casual attitude toward dress in the workplace, it would be a mistake to underdress as a school or district leader. Jeans, tank tops, flip-flops and athletic attire, just don't cut it. Here are some common sense tips regarding professional attire as an educational leader:

- When presenting to parents, teachers or the community wear a suit. If you want people to think you are in charge, wear a suit. If you want to be perceived as a professional leader, wear a suit.

- Whatever you choose to wear at work, remember most of all you must feel comfortable; it's a long day. Just don't get crazy and think that the latest fashion trends will add dimension to your leadership style. They won't.

## 8.  FORGIVE ME

On any given day you won't go without hearing someone say I'm *sorry*. Most leaders view saying *I'm sorry* as a way to keep them on good terms with people and believe it helps to build relationships with their workers. Researchers, however, indicate that leaders who use the apology ritual to establish or restore emotional balance in a conversation are actually perceived by employees as weak or in a "one down" position. When people apologize it is usually an expression of regret for having done something wrong to another. Unfortunately, leaders are harder on themselves when it comes to accepting or taking on blame. One main reason to avoid apologizing at work is that it tends to put you in an inferior position. Another thing to keep in mind is that it's not necessary to apologize over situations in which you have no control. For example, if the sprinklers go off unexpectedly and people get drenched coming in from the parking lot, it is sufficient to state whatever the problem is minus any apologies followed by recommendations to fix it.

If you want to check your speech on any given day, you would be amazed at how many times you use the words *I'm sorry* in your speech. This apologetic ritual is hard to break but can be done with a bit of practice. Become aware of when, where, and the number of times you use *I'm sorry* in one given day. Create a plan to reduce your *sorry habit* by trying to catch yourself each time you utter *I'm sorry*. Try substituting the phrase, *excuse me*. This replacement is not half as bad as an apology and will lessen your weakened power position. Saying *I'm sorry* every time you present important information or apologizing for speaking can be deadly in the workplace. Once you become aware of this nasty habit your ability to overcome it will be even easier.

## 9. DIVERSITY IS NOT A NOUN

We all have learned diversity comes in many shapes and sizes, such as language, gender, religion, poverty, health, parenting issues, and the list goes on. We also know that it is extremely important for leaders to continually embrace individual differences.

When someone questions my integrity about a certain issue, I won't go there. I won't allow myself to be put in a corner having to defend my position or my beliefs. Whenever the opportunity to speak is available and appropriate, I share my overriding philosophy of respecting the cultural and individual differences of all people. This is very important. As a leader, by openly sharing your diversity philosophy with all stakeholder groups, you set the tone for a district or school.

In addition to publicly announcing that I embraced diversity, I continually worked with district administrators and support staff to review and modify policies and programs that reflect issues of growing diversity. Follow through with your beliefs.

For example, as a superintendent I worked in a school district with a 12 percent African American student population, yet out of 500 teachers, only four were African American. It's easy to spout off about valuing diversity but if you don't "put your money where your mouth is" you end up looking like a hypocrite. I made it my goal to recruit more racially diverse teachers after learning about these low numbers.

On another occasion, I learned that my neighbor, a Mexican gardener, had been turned down three times for one of four open groundskeeper positions in our district. Upon further investigation, I learned that all 10 district gardeners were white, one being the son-in law of our Assistant Superintendent. When asked why Juan was not hired, district human resources informed me that he didn't speak English very well in his interview. "Why would a gardener need perfect English?" I asked. I continued to push; "Over 50% of our student population is Hispanic and not one gardener in this district is Hispanic? And Juan is a gardener by trade?" Everyone sensed how enraged I was becoming. The next week the Director of Grounds informed me that he was interviewing some new groundkeeper applicants for an open position and [good news] Juan was on the interview list. Three weeks later, as I was leaving my office, I spotted Juan, standing high up on a ladder trimming trees. I looked up and he caught my eye. He smiled, I winked.

## 10.   ONE FOR THE ROAD

As a school administrator, I've seen it all when it comes to alcohol. I've seen a superintendent at a retreat having too much to drink and slobbering over his dinner, losing respect from almost every administrator in the room. I've observed a principal arriving for prom duty smelling of alcohol and eventually losing his job after several parent complaints. I've known several superintendents who were arrested for DUI, later losing their administrative credentials in addition to being dismissed from the job.

With the internet, parents and employees can also pull up a person's criminal and traffic record at any time. As the authors of this book we can't stress enough that it doesn't pay to have a drink out in public with your employees. And it certainly doesn't pay to have a drink out in public when you have parents, students or community members in attendance.

If you must drink, drink at home, drink on the weekend, but avoid drinking in public.

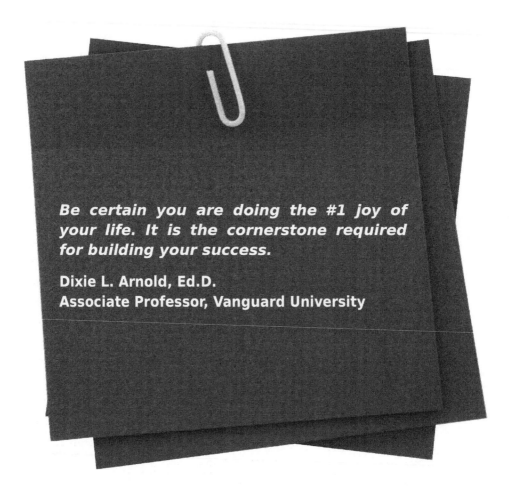

*Be certain you are doing the #1 joy of your life. It is the cornerstone required for building your success.*

**Dixie L. Arnold, Ed.D.**
**Associate Professor, Vanguard University**

## 11. NEVER MISS A GOOD CHANCE TO SHUT UP

The majority in top leadership positions love to talk; in fact we talk so much I think we like to hear the sound of our own voices. As you know, there are critical speaking engagements such as convocations, award ceremonies, strategic planning sessions and board meetings where we must talk. But the most important part of being an effective leader involves the fine art of *learning to listen*.

So how does one engage in this activity of listening when our role involves so much talking, offering advice, directing people, solving problems and giving orders? Listening is not an easy skill. Listening is also not a passive process and takes practice. A primary technique for how to listen to employees involves your willingness to have an open mind and be open to hearing different sides of an issue.

For example, whenever I participated in teacher negotiations, it was important to sit silently and listen to what teachers were actually saying. It became painfully obvious that it was very difficult for me to throw away my bias toward an issue during these sessions. Once I learned how to work through this stumbling block, I was able to get at the heart and soul of what teachers really wanted negotiated; more respect, less top down decisions, more supplies, or more collaboration. All of these concerns would have been difficult to unveil had I not listened to their entire message. This allowed me to weigh my thoughts against what was said, and then finally respond to them.

Interesting, when you try to listen you cannot be the judge since your mind can only process so much. It is also imperative as a leader to recognize that effective listening does not always equate to an agreement of what is being stated. Rather, artful listening merely communicates to the speaker a willingness to communicate.

One of the most difficult habits that can block artful listening is that of not holding back on your urge to jump into the conversation to voice your own opinion. Researchers believe the root of this urge stems from our ego, in that we believe what we have to say is more important than what the speaker is saying. It's critical when listening to gauge a good time for your input, as you don't want it to be perceived as an interruption. However, if you catch yourself jumping into a conversation with the words, *YES BUT...* then beware... you are NOT listening. *YES BUT* responses... mean that you can't help yourself and should be a warning sign that you need to work on improving your listening techniques. In addition to curbing your *YES BUTS*, try to employ visual cues such as nodding your head, leaning forward, making eye contact, taking notes and offering affirmative "uh ha" responses to show the speaker you are listening.

These tactics are a good first step to artful listening. You'd be surprised at how much you can learn, when you learn to listen to your stakeholders.

## 12. BOOTS ON THE GROUND

When we sign on to serve as educational leaders, it becomes self-evident that students, schools, and entire school districts can take precedence over our personal well-being and are often considered our *second families*. Take note and don't get caught up in an emergency at school or district office without first having a backup plan.

For example, I loved wearing high heels at work; they made me feel ten feet tall and I believed they made me look more powerful as a woman in a position of authority. I soon discovered that in an emergency, these high heels had to go. I realized one needed two things to survive a workplace emergency; a backup set of [comfortable] clothes and a plan to alert my family that I wasn't coming home from work as anticipated.

Learning to be prepared for emergencies came the hard way for me. One day I left campus to grab a fruit smoothie for lunch and while driving, the entire drink fell in my lap. I was drenched. I was panicked because I had an important teacher meeting that afternoon. I knew there was no way I could walk on campus with smoothie fluid dripping down my outfit. My first thought was to run to Walmart and purchase a dry pair of pants, but time was getting short and I needed to attend an important meeting.

As a mom of four I quickly went to Plan B, thinking I might get lucky and find some spare clothing in my Suburban and I did... a brand new pair of boys "skater" pants purchased for my son earlier in the week that I planned to return. Desperate, I put them on and returned to school. Fortunately, my teachers were good sports about the incident, kidding me about my pants and calling me "skater" for the day; it was actually pretty funny.

Take note; maintain a second set of professional AND casual

clothing at work. Throughout my tenure as a school administrator I knew to stash away some Nikes, loose fitting shirts and comfortable pants and warm jackets in a back room for when I least expected it, such as our meningitis outbreak, guns found on campus, city flooding that left all roads impassable, and the firing of our head football coach.

## 13. UNDER MY THUMB

P eople can work *for you* and better yet, *with you*, but avoid saying that people work *under you*.

As a superintendent I mentored a promising young administrator who made many mistakes along the way but always took the opportunity to learn from them. He later became a school superintendent. One night, early in his career, I watched him lose big points with his team as he delivered an important technology presentation to the Board of Trustees. Over several hundred district employees heard him proudly thank those who had worked hard to make the new technology plan a reality. He followed up the board presentation by enthusiastically stating, "I would like to thank *those who worked under me* for their time and effort extended on this project."

The crowd visual still haunts me today as I vividly recall how several of his *underlings* grimaced in disgust. As his mentor, I took him aside the next day and coached him on his communication *faux pas*. As a result he learned it is important to communicate that he is part of a bigger team grander than himself.

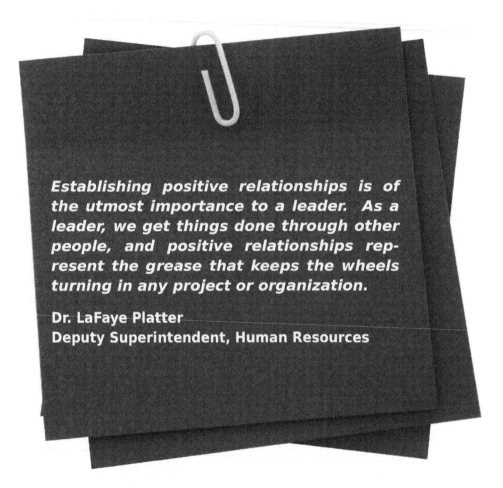

*Establishing positive relationships is of the utmost importance to a leader. As a leader, we get things done through other people, and positive relationships represent the grease that keeps the wheels turning in any project or organization.*

**Dr. LaFaye Platter**
**Deputy Superintendent, Human Resources**

## 14. DO THE RIGHT THING

E very leader is familiar with the Warren G. Bennis quote that declares, "Managers do things right. Leaders do the right thing."

As educational leaders we all face ethical challenges almost daily. Whether it is a released employee asking for a letter of recommendation, a parent requesting a schedule change because of their child's teacher's sexual orientation or a board member demanding you hire their relative, you will find yourself in ethical situations that are often politically charged.

Know that as a leader, almost *everything has political ramifications*. When I teach ethical leadership to aspiring administrators, students tend to always give the "right" answer to ethical dilemmas. Sure, knowing the "right" answer to ethical dilemmas and decision making is important, but executing the ethical actions that align to your values and beliefs is even more paramount... and this easier said than done. The nuances of ethical leadership, including organizational culture and political dynamics, will often be the invisible factors that will tempt you to justify an unethical decision.

BEWARE!! If your superintendent asks you to sign off on an illegal and unethical financial transaction, what would you do? This is one area you do not want to compromise, even if doing the "right" thing costs you your job. Although making an ethical decision may be unpopular and land you in political hot water, the ramifications are usually temporary. However, the consequences of making an unethical decision can haunt you for a lifetime.

## 15.   SURVEY QUEEN

S urvey the wisdom of your people. What a thought. As a leader it's easy to get sidetracked by those who speak the most and the loudest. Sometimes we think their "roar" is the most important thing of all and tend to overreact to their protests.

During my first year as a rookie principal overseeing 60 middle school teachers and an equal number of support staff, three teachers continued to seize my attention. I should have listened to my father's advice more seriously before taking on my first real leadership role. He cautioned me, suggesting I take notes on my first day on the job. "Remember the names of those who are first to arrive in your office," he advised. "There's a good chance they will be your most difficult employees."

How right he was. The first three teachers all came with smiles, congratulations, and big requests. The first said, "I'm glad you're here," he smiled, "We need someone like you to take student discipline seriously around here."

My second greeter, the most veteran teacher on staff, wasn't so friendly. "You need to look at the duty schedule," he snarled. "All the new teachers have the best schedules. Just look, you'll see."

My last visitor of the morning was my favorite; she brought me a flower arrangement from her garden as a welcome gift. "Don't take the staff too seriously," she advised. "These people are a bunch of whiners and will eat you alive if you let them." I knew the school had a fractured history, but this woman's depiction of the situation was over the top.

Over the next few weeks it became clear to me that my father wasn't kidding. These three greeters were a major problem. During faculty meetings they would speak the loudest and attempt to give the impression they were communicating for the entire staff. Whenever I presented a new school policy one of them would jump up and disagree, and then share an opinion of the situation; of course it was always counter to my latest proposal. For example, I developed a new duty schedule that would afford teachers more prep time; these three dissented in unison, "What are you thinking? This won't work," and of course they had backup data to support their claim. After a few months, their complaints started to wear me out.

In the beginning, I didn't know how to respond to them during staff meetings, mainly because no other staff members would speak up against them. As I look back, I think they were what we call "Bully Teachers." Speak loud, carry a big stick and you'll get your way.

Out of desperation, I began to survey the staff on several contentious items. I was amazed when the survey results were tabulated; only eight out of 60 teachers thought the new duty schedule was a disaster. The majority of teachers stated they were willing to try the different schedule to see if it was more effective than one they were currently using.

During the next faculty meeting I printed out the survey results and presented them to the entire staff. My three greeters sat silent with disgust on their faces. Over time I learned other creative ways to deal with the bully teacher mentality but the survey method was my favorite.

As my leadership skills grew over time, I learned that the survey tool was a powerful way to determine if programs, people, and resource allocations were meeting student needs. As a superintendent, I administered a survey to all employees requesting a rating of my leadership. The results were stunning; not only did I learn that people thought I was exceeding district expectations, but I was able to use the opposing results to target areas of improvement. One area revealed that the majority surveyed believed I needed to create more advisory teams to gather employee input.

Later, at our management retreat, I presented the survey results and afterward had an honest and open dialogue with everyone in attendance. After the retreat, a formal "Executive Summary" explaining a simplified version of the results was written and disseminated to all district stakeholders. In retrospect, this risky act of surveying employees to assess my leadership skills was one of the more powerful actions ever taken to demonstrate my trustworthiness and commitment an educational leader.

# 16. SMALL CRIMES

Think twice before charging something to the district credit card that could later cause embarrassment. I have known several leaders that used the district credit card to allegedly get them out of a jam. One principal charged a full tank of gas to the district credit card, claiming he didn't have his own card on hand. "I just forgot to pay the district back," he said. "I had good intentions. I just forgot..., what's the big deal?"

Another district administrator charged his wife's acupressure to the card, confessing that he thought the expense could be justified if he didn't claim mileage on his conference expense report.

Another colleague used the district credit card to buy a round of drinks for his management team at a conference. "I planned to reimburse the alcohol charges back to the district in cash when I returned, but forgot," he said apologetically.

Now here's the deal. First, if you plan to charge personal expenses to the district credit card or fudge conference reimbursement claim forms with the intent to pay them back later, plan on losing a ton of leadership points or losing your job altogether. Those working in the business department never hear the full story and love to gossip that you are milking the district and should not be trusted. Second, if you are in charge of authorizing employee credit card and conference expenditures, you might want to think twice about keeping administrators on board who push the limits. This type of poor leadership judgment in an organization is unacceptable and should not be tolerated. If you turn a blind eye and condemn this indiscretion your reputation will also be tainted throughout the district.

## 17.    EARLY BIRD

It's extremely critical that the people you lead think you are serious about your job. Showing up for work early sets the tone when folks come to work and see that you are already there and deeply immersed in your role; taking care of meetings, conversing with people, sending out important emails, etc.

While you may not be the last person to leave at the end of the day... it's very important as a leader to arrive to work early and get a lot of the small problems of the day taken care of in advance.

Additionally, Murphy's Law often will take effect during these times. It will be the morning you are NOT there early when something will go wrong, a student is hit in the crosswalk, a fight occurs on a bus, or an irate parent threatens a teacher. Believe me, word will get out there was no principal on campus and people will be looking for answers.

## 18. SICK AND TIRED

Use your rational thinking head, and stay home if you are coughing, sneezing or sick with the flu. While your non-exempt status as a leader may allow comp time for missing work, other employees may not be so fortunate. Missing work for them could mean the loss of a day's pay. If you must come to work sick, for whatever reason, make sure you have no obvious nose-running symptoms.

You may believe you're doing people a favor by coming to work, but most people think it's a bigger favor if you stay home. If circumstances force you to come to work sick (emergency situation or important crisis meeting that can't be cancelled) make every effort to contain your germs. We all know that sickness can come on at any time, but it's best not to have people see you in this weakened state. Most people like to think that their leader is invincible.

Remember if you are mildly ill, sick to death, or just plain miserable, people may perceive you as weak and/or heartless for coming to work. It's a no-win situation so do the right thing and stay home and get well. Be mindful of your employees by showing that you are a considerate and responsible leader.

---

Excerpts from *Rules of the Game: How to Win a Job in Educational Leadership*
Delmar Publishing, 2012

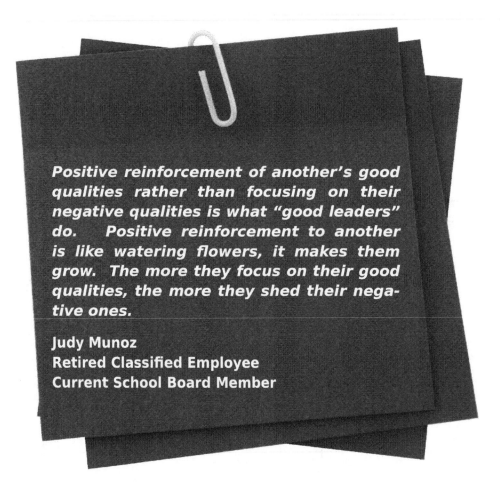

*Positive reinforcement of another's good qualities rather than focusing on their negative qualities is what "good leaders" do. Positive reinforcement to another is like watering flowers, it makes them grow. The more they focus on their good qualities, the more they shed their negative ones.*

Judy Munoz
Retired Classified Employee
Current School Board Member

# 19.  LAST MAN STANDING

S ometimes it can be just as important to be the last man standing as it is to be the "early bird." We all know that being an educational leader is not a 9-5 job. Whether you are a cabinet member at a late night Board Meeting or a principal supervising a school dance, the hours can be long and exhausting.

I remember being a new site administrator and adjusting to the grueling schedule at the high school level. After working eight hours during the school day and three hours of sport supervision, I found myself, along with the rest of the administrative team, supervising a dance that went on until midnight. At the conclusion of the dance, we all proceeded to the parking lot to supervise students getting picked up by parents. As more and more students left the campus, my boss started sending members of the administrative team home. The closer it came to 1 a.m., the louder the voices in my head yelled, "Pick me! Pick me!" but my inner cries fell on deaf ears. The voices only intensified as I realized I could no longer feel my feet and was shivering in the cold night weather. Then finally it happened... I heard my name, I thought at first I was becoming delusional from lack of sleep, but no, I heard it, my boss called my name and I was released from duty to go home, and HE became the last man standing. That night my boss became my hero and that one gesture would pay dividends as we worked together as a team throughout the next few years.

It's definitely lonely at the top, and by that you must remember that as the leader you will often be required to stay late and perhaps even overnight during an emergency or crisis board meeting. You cannot toss this responsibility over to an assistant; if a board is meeting late, you will be required to stay. It's just that simple. As principal I was in charge of taking all of our 450 eighth graders to an all-day Disneyland promotion activity scheduled from noon until midnight. We had an elaborate strategy for how students would return to the buses at the end of the event and were confident we had thought of everything to make this a foolproof plan. By 12:45 a.m. every student had been accounted for except one. I was exhausted from a very long day and wanted desperately to get home and get some sleep.

The next day would prove to be even more demanding than this one with promotional ceremonies on the docket. We grilled several of her friends who "thought maybe" they saw the student with her boyfriend; a 21-year-old from another state who met her inside Disneyland. You know how this story ends. I called her father to apprise him of the situation but he sounded too inebriated to drive to Disneyland and couldn't offer up any suggestions for locating his daughter. The buses took off without the student.

Our backup plan involved having the principal (that's me) drive her own car, just in case someone did not return to the buses. I then called the police, who arrived an hour later. I spotted the student coming out of the park alone. She made a modest attempt to head toward the parking lot where the buses were once parked. I wasn't very pleasant and informed her that she would not be attending any more promotional activities, among other things. By that time, her father managed to find a ride to Disneyland with his older son.

What a mess, what drama. If you have ever served in a leadership role, I suspect you have found yourself in a similar late night situation, tired, hungry, and short-tempered. Remember, when you are the boss, and in charge, you will be the one held accountable. You will be the last man or woman standing.

# 20. FENG SHUI

F eng Shui is an ancient Chinese philosophy of nature focused on living in harmony with our environment. One of the small things I often observed in the workplace, but had not often considered, is how people arrange and use their office space.

As an administrator, your office will likely be a hub of activity. At times it may be a place where a staff member shares their joy about a new baby or the sadness over the loss of a parent. You will also likely have student and staff disciplinary conferences, informal chats with parents and teachers and, at times, highly confidential meetings.

Knowing how to arrange the space and then use it to your advantage can be key in setting the tone in your office. One of the first items of business I undertook upon assuming a new administrative job was to rearrange my office. Symbolically it signifies a change in leadership. You will not be sitting in Dr. So and So's office, it will be your own.

In my office I had a traditional desk with two visitor's chairs, an industrial couch and a small round table and chairs. Depending on the purpose of a visit to my office, I would use one of the three areas. On occasions where it was necessary to be the "leader" and the one in power, I would strategically sit behind my desk and people would sit across from me. If I was comforting someone, I would either sit next to them in a chair or on the couch to increase my proximity to show I cared.

Lastly, if I was collaborating with an individual or small group, I used the round table. The tendency to have an autocratic office set-up, that of the typical boss sitting behind the desk, is no longer considered effective in modern day leadership. Rather the collaborative approach with round tables, and face to face interaction has become very common to help promote a positive and collective leadership spirit.

## 21.   A WORD FROM YOUR SPONSOR

W hen taking on the challenge to serve as an educational leader, or for that matter, if you are thinking about moving ahead in your career, it's essential to work with selected mentors and sponsors. Many people have shared that they were hesitant to approach me for career advice because of my busy schedule as a superintendent. Quite frankly, they thought they would be a burden. What they didn't know was that personally, it was almost impossible to turn them down.

Don't be afraid to take a chance and ask someone you trust to serve as your mentor. Most of us remember the hurdles we jumped through to gain our current jobs and remain successful, and many of us are enthusiastic about helping our colleagues. But again, you can't get help if you don't ask. Although asking for help is hard for some, it may be the most important step you will take on your journey to grow as a leader.

Finding a sponsor is another matter. Every leader needs a sponsor, a person to publically promote and speak well of them in public. A sponsor is the person in your corner who says things like, "Our new superintendent is amazing; I worked with her on the last project and she gets things done." Another sponsor remark might sound like, "John is the best principal for our high school. It won't be long before he's our next superintendent."

Sponsors are people who support your initiatives and promote your projects. They advocate on your behalf, often having the ability to connect you to important players and jobs. In doing so, they make themselves look good. And precisely because sponsors take a risk with you, they expect you to be a star performer and extremely loyal to them.

Sponsors know who you are and what you stand for because you have taken the time to get to know them and keep them apprised of your latest projects and accomplishments.

Finding a mentor is easy; all you have to do is ask someone and they usually take on the role; it's a relatively loose relationship. Your mentor will serve as a sounding board or a shoulder to cry on, offering advice and support as needed and guidance as requested; they expect very little in return. You cannot ask someone to be your sponsor. Sponsors are much more vested in their disciples than mentors, offering guidance and critical feedback because they believe in you.

A sponsor is someone who will go to bat for you, and wouldn't necessarily be your friend, but rather someone you admire on a professional level. As a leader it will be important for you to consider those you can tap as both mentors and sponsors to help you grow, learn and thrive in your career.

## 22. WHEN THE EXTRAORDINARY BECOMES ORDINARY

If you are anything like me, you like to exceed people's expectations. Since I was a child I have always had this tendency. Whether it was building a four foot tall Valentine's Day box, winning the pumpkin carving contest or landing the lead in the school play, I always strived for excellence.

As a teacher and school administrator, these tendencies followed me. Presentations to Cabinet went well above expectations and were often accompanied with a glossy folder containing 10 pages of additional handouts and yearly goal setting morphed into a three year, color coded, excel spreadsheet with clip art.

After years of doing this, I started to realize my once "extraordinary" efforts were now viewed as "ordinary" by some of those around me. *Extraordinary was now my new norm.*

Although this may sound like a positive disposition, I learned a few important lessons about being "extraordinary." First, being extraordinary is not as fulfilling when everyone expects it from you; second, eventually there is nowhere else to go. You will likely hit the ceiling by your own doing; and third, and most importantly, you lose sight of the "ordinary" things around you... a child's smile, the smell of freshly cut grassy fields, a parent's hug in appreciation, a brief conversation in the hall, a simple thank you email and the knowledge you make a difference in so many people's lives... now that's Extraordinary!

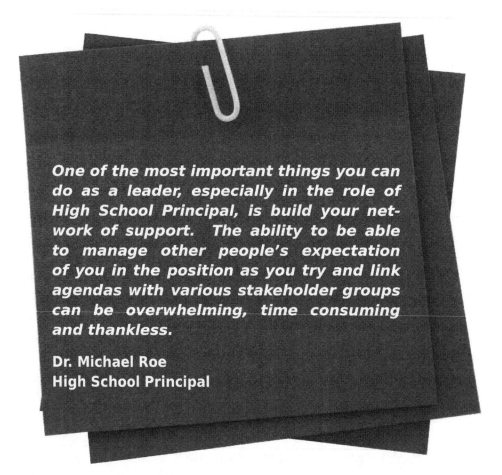

*One of the most important things you can do as a leader, especially in the role of High School Principal, is build your network of support. The ability to be able to manage other people's expectation of you in the position as you try and link agendas with various stakeholder groups can be overwhelming, time consuming and thankless.*

**Dr. Michael Roe**
**High School Principal**

## 23. HONOR THE PAST, EMBRACE THE FUTURE

O ne of the biggest rookie mistakes one can make is to take the helm of an organization and not honor existing traditions. Traditions are what build culture and group cohesion. Just think, discarding a long held tradition in your organization is like taking Christmas away from a five-year-old. Don't do it!

Showing your stakeholders that you honor and embrace their existing traditions sends a very powerful message and will earn you major points. As the principal of a new school with a new leadership team, I soon learned that the school had a yearly pancake breakfast in December to show staff appreciation. The administrative team and counselors would cook every year. While I wasn't enamored with the idea of a pancake breakfast, I thought I'd wait and see how it went before making any changes.

My first year there, I found a gift bag on my desk. Inside was an apron with the school logo and my name embroidered on it. Receiving the apron was my rite of passage and was the school's way of inviting me to be part of their existing tradition. I still have my apron to this day.

Had I come in as the new leader and canceled this tradition, and replaced it with an idea of my own, I would have offended and dishonored my staff. Find out what the traditions are at your school/district and become a part of them. You can always start your new traditions as you honor the past and embrace the future of a school or district.

## 24.   THERE IS AN APP FOR THAT

It has never been more important than now to be tech savvy as an educational leader. Today's 21$^{st}$ century schools call for 21$^{st}$ century leaders. In addition to today's students, who have never known a world without internet and social media, many in the current workforce are also digital natives. There is an expectation school leaders should know and leverage technology as part of their role as the instructional leaders.

Technology has changed the way we do school business and as the leader, you need to be seen as being tech savvy. Here are four areas to ensure you can function in a technology driven environment:

### 1.  Social Media
Many of your stakeholders do the majority of their communication and maintain an online presence through social media. You need to "join" them there. Many schools and districts now have Facebook pages or Twitter accounts. A school or district account can positively promote the great things happening in your organization.

### 2.  Work Productivity
Your SMART phone is only going to be as smart as you are! As leaders, we know there is never enough time in a day to get everything done. Your phone can be either your nemesis or your best friend. Learn how to use it to your best advantage.

### 3. Instructional Technology

You cannot expect your staff to use technology if you are not conversant with these applications yourself. Take the time to learn different types of technology and incorporate them in your next staff meeting. This will go a long way and send a message that you understand what is being expected of those in the trenches.

### 4. Communication

We all know communication is rapidly changing. Survey your staff to determine their preferences for communicating. For many, their communication preference will be email and/or text messaging. Learn how to effectively communicate with both.

## 25.  THE UNEXPECTED DEATH OF A STUDENT

P lanning in advance for the death of a student is not a pleasant activity, but as a leader responsible for children, it is
critical to have a simple strategy to follow if a child dies under
your watch.

Write out an emergency plan and place it on your tablet,
iPhone or desk. The plan should include people's names and telephone numbers to immediately refer to such as pastors, police
liaisons, community partners, counselors, or florists. While your
school district may already have a student "Crisis Team" in place,
it's important to have this contact information readily available.
Another part of the plan should list out specific district/school
protocols for this type of emergency; who to inform, sample parent letters, staff messages, etc.

As a school superintendent I experienced the death of too
many children. My first encounter caught me short and I had to
rely on pure instinct to assist our families, employees, and students. There is no simple formula for this type of crisis interven-
tion, but having a "to do" list in advance can help since it's easy
to forget how to respond during a tragedy.

I will never forget the day our district suffered through the
horrific death of two students. Two of our second graders were
involved in a fatal car accident on their way to school after being
broadsided by a farmer's truck. Even though an emergency plan
existed, my assistant superintendent had to prompt me to reach
out to the poor grieving parents "in person" the next day. I was
grateful to have a partner on my leadership team that could
assist me through the tragedy.

On another occasion, in my role as assistant superintendent,
our elementary school became paralyzed after two fourth grade

twin brothers were fatally shot by their stepfather over the weekend. On Monday morning, the superintendent was in his office creating a communication plan for the community, which seemed like a good crisis protocol. I recall walking into his office that morning to inquire about his plan to visit the school to express condolences and offer support. He informed me that the principal was "in charge" of the school and that she could handle the crisis. He ended our conversation by suggesting that I could spend the day at the site if I really wanted to help.

I followed his advice and counseled as many families, support staff, teachers and students as humanly possible throughout the day and several to follow. The most difficult task of all was having to remove the twin's belongings from their desks in each classroom as requested by their grieving mother. Fortunately, grief counselors remained in each classroom throughout the day to help the boys' classmates express their grief. One thing that sticks in my mind about that horrible week to this day was the question that people kept asking; "When do you think the superintendent will be here?" For me, his absence as a leader was unforgivable.

As a site administrator, being prepared for a death on campus is equally important. As an assistant principal I was the second adult on the scene after one of our male students collapsed during a pick-up game of football after school. Our athletic trainer was assessing the student's vitals and immediately started CPR. I contacted the office to call 911 and began clearing the growing crowd of students gathered to watch the situation and attempted to clear a path for the paramedics.

It is very easy to freeze under pressure. Remain calm and stay focused on the immediate needs of the injured student, and then attend to any students who may have witnessed the incident and may be traumatized. I ensured that someone on site would accompany the child to the hospital and directed our counselor to ride in the ambulance and asked our bilingual assistant principal to follow the ambulance to the hospital. Sadly, the young man died that day. It was a helpless feeling and one I will never forget. Our counselor actually had the difficult task of breaking the news to the young man's family. In the days that followed, we convened our crisis counselors to support students in expressing their grief and hosted a memorial video presentation in the school library. We also ensured that all employees were consoled in addition to urging anyone in need to avail themselves of district sponsored counseling services.

As you know from your educational studies in grief counseling, it is important that the counselors provide unlimited opportunities for students to express their grief over the loss of a school mate. As a superintendent, we lost a popular football player during spring vacation. He and his friend were playing "chicken" with a freight train and through sheer foolishness the student was stuck by the train, killing him instantly. It is one thing to have access to school resources when navigating a crisis, but to lose a student during vacation is another story. When word traveled throughout the community that this popular student had died, students from everywhere began to congregate on the train tracks in response. Even though students were persuaded to leave the tracks by their parents and school administrators, they would not listen to reason; at one time the media reported over 350 students were gathered on the tracks. It was an extremely dangerous situation.

Parents called me for help. I was already at the district office working with available staff during the vacation period who were willing to help during this difficult situation. It had also been reported that one student had attempted suicide on his own as a result of his sorrow. Things were getting out of control. During my first two years as a superintendent I made some good connections with the local clergymen in town and felt comfortable phoning one pastor for help. He was well known throughout the youth community for being a hip and cool guy. He instantly offered to donate his congregation's newly built church center as a meeting area and indicated that students could spend as much time there as they needed. After giving him the go ahead, he drove out to the tracks in an attempt to convince our students to leave. Standing high on the back of his truck, bullhorn in hand, he managed to persuade the group to meet back at his church. One by one, students headed to the church. Parents were relieved he was able to encourage everyone off the tracks and many volunteered their time to work alongside the pastor to provide additional support. For nearly four straight days, this sole pastor coordinated ceremonies, speeches, and grief counseling for students, family, and community. While the deceased child was a member of a neighboring church, final memorial services were held in this pastor's church. The grieving parents were extremely grateful for the community and faith-based support and felt it was the right decision to have their son's memorial at this particular church. Finally students and families were able to gain a sense of closure.

In times of extreme crisis, such as the unexpected death of a student, remember that effective leaders must plan in advance, not be afraid to lean on their team for support and reach out to the community for additional resources.

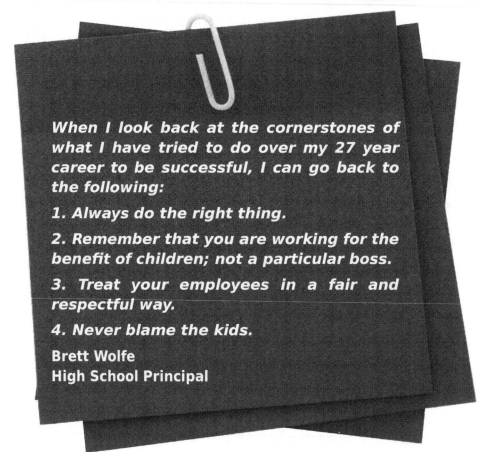

*When I look back at the cornerstones of what I have tried to do over my 27 year career to be successful, I can go back to the following:*

*1. Always do the right thing.*

*2. Remember that you are working for the benefit of children; not a particular boss.*

*3. Treat your employees in a fair and respectful way.*

*4. Never blame the kids.*

**Brett Wolfe**
**High School Principal**

## 26. THE WORLD ACCORDING TO A SPIRAL NOTEBOOK

One important strategy that I employed as a leader is that of keeping a small spiral notebook on my desk when conversing on the phone or sitting in a meeting. I would "capture" the conversation by writing down simple notes to help remember names, dates, and important details. It can be a blessing to have all these notes in one place if a situation arises in which you are requested to recall what happened on a particular day, restate a person's response to a question, or recollect important details such as attendance numbers or projected revenues.

By keeping and maintaining a private spiral notebook, you can easily refer back to your notes and look like a pro. I used this strategy during meetings by writing down people's names, jotting down the meeting's purpose and summarizing results. Sometimes during a meeting I would forget the person's name, which could be rather embarrassing, but not to worry, I could easily check my notes and begin to call them by their name again in the conversation.

The spiral notebook tactic not only helps with memory issues and recall of important information weeks or months later, but adds to your credibly as a caring and interested leader. People tend to think you are taking an honest interest in them when they see you writing down something they said. Also, don't forget to date your conversations; more than once I was asked to recall a specific date for an attorney and knew it was right there in my spiral notebook.

I know some of you may be thinking, "Really, a spiral notebook? Aren't we in the 21st century?" In most instances, we would advocate for the use of technology to help streamline your work. However, in this case, during most conversations and meetings it is still socially unacceptable to take notes electronically. Additionally it's not wise to have certain confidential notes kept on your district computer as they may contain sensitive information.

# 27.  FAIR PLAY

When you hear the word *accountability* you may want to reflect upon how you will encourage others to follow your leadership without experiencing a *Mutiny on the Bounty* scenario. Ask yourself, "How will you hold people accountable, delegate authority, assign responsibly, and maintain accountably?"

Too many times, when trying to help employees improve their performance, they will come back and express that no one ever tried to help them or that they never knew a specific duty was part of their job. As a superintendent, I was always stunned when terminated employees took legal action against the district because they claimed no one offered them help to improve, when that just wasn't true. So it's important to share with employees exactly how you are providing support when helping them to improve. Some important pointers to support you in this area include:

### 1. Assign responsibility
Ensure that your employees know their roles and responsibilities of the job. It's hard to help people improve or expect greatness from them when they don't know what they are supposed to be doing.

### 2. Delegate
Learn to delegate to others and subtly share your power. You have to assume that the people you hired can do the job. If they fall short, that's when you step in to provide support.

### 3. Support

Your job as a leader is to provide support and let people know you are there to help them when necessary. Disciplined employees can get the upper hand when confronted with poor performance that was not documented; for example: *"You never told me what to do or how to improve in this area and you didn't give me any help."*

### 4. Monitor

Use "management by walking around" and regular conferences to assess if people are doing what you expect of them.

## 28. PEACE OF MIND

One of the hardest calls you will ever make as an educational leader is to call Child Protective Services (CPS). To know or believe a child is in danger is devastating.

My colleague, a school principal, was approached by his assistant coach, who reported that he saw the head coach of one of the high profile sports teams punch a player in the stomach. Sounds like a no-brainer right? Of course! However, there were a few more details that complicated the manner. The student the head coach punched was not only a player on the team, but was also his own son. The coach argued that it was a private family manner.

The principal reported the incident to CPS, setting the community in an uproar and shortly thereafter the coach was placed on leave. The other players and parents were outraged and wanted their beloved coach back. Teachers on campus questioned the principal's actions and soon the situation became very political, involving the School Board and legal counsel. Toward the end of the ordeal it seemed as if the principal was the guilty one.

Despite this, the principal does not regret his decision to report. When it comes to the safety and well-being of children, nothing else matters.

It is your responsibility to report any suspected neglect and/or abuse. It is the child protective agency's responsibility to investigate and make a determination if there was neglect or abuse. Do not hesitate to call 911 and CPS. Doing so will always be in everyone's best interest, including your own.

## 29.   LEADERS ARE CLOSER THAN THEY APPEAR

E very book on leadership touts the cardinal rule for success; that of visibility. People want to see their leaders in the flesh, not imagine them sitting at a desk, behind closed doors. They want to see their leaders visible on campus, walking school hallways, spending time in classrooms and donating significant time in the community.

Following through on this cardinal rule, however, is easier said than done. I've known many administrators who followed this leadership axiom to the max, spending most of their time visiting schools and classrooms while important *behind the desk* tasks were neglected. They soon found that in their absence things began to fall apart back at the district. Conversely, I've known administrators that didn't know how to manage their time effectively and were never seen at appropriate times or expected venues. These leaders were perceived as *leaderless leaders* by the rank and file and many even thought they didn't care about the students. As always, there should be a happy medium regarding one's visibility as a leader.

Effective leaders should be aware of compulsory attendance at Open Houses, Back to School Nights, certain student performances and award nights. Those dates should be calendared and equally shared with your leadership team and staff. It is important to *share the wealth* with high profile events and not believe that you must take on every event yourself.

A leader's stamina and longevity decreases over time, especially when spending 3-4 nights a week out on special assignment, or for that matter, working 60-70 hour weeks. Collaborate with your leadership team, assistant principals, district office directors and support staff to decide who will attend which events in advance. Unless it's an extremely important activity, it doesn't make sense to have both the principal and assistant principal or superintendent and deputy superintendent attend the same meetings when it should only take one leader to manage or serve as the head representative. Make good use of everyone's valuable time.

Another strategy to increase your visibility factor is to schedule classroom or school visitations on your calendar in advance. These visits don't have to be long. A high-value visibility opportunity exists every morning when parents, students, and staff arrive to school.

As a principal I could be found standing by the school's main gate greeting students and parents. I informed my secretary not to schedule parent meetings during this important time unless it was a dire emergency. Twenty years later, people still remark about my presence at the front gate, taking time to acknowledge parents and students.

As a superintendent I also knew how to target high-value attendance opportunities and I was well known for devoting 3-4 days a week to visiting schools and talking with staff and students as they arrived in the morning. This important school "face time" not only gave me credibility and respect, but afforded me that informal time to learn what was happening at each school. Before leaving, I always dropped in on the cafeteria staff and custodians to thank them for a job well done.

Additionally, I tried to coordinate visits with sporting events while working in a high school district that scheduled nonstop, around-the-clock athletic activities. In one afternoon, I would visit a baseball game to say hello to the team, attend a soccer game, converse with parents at the Booster Snack Shack window, drive to a track meet to wish students well, and finally, sit with proud parents in the bleachers to watch the last five minutes of our winning girls' volleyball game. All of these parents were gratified to have the superintendent present at their children's events.

It's about timing and the political factor. It is essential to be visible as a leader; it's also important to know your limitations; be aware of events that are *known show stoppers* and recognize that too little or too much face time can damage a leader's credibility and effectiveness.

## 30. THEY LIKE ME, THEY REALLY LIKE ME

If you want to be liked, don't go into educational leadership. Your job is to make good decisions for children, which is not always an easy task. Most people will support your decisions if you use good judgment and follow decent decision-making protocols.

Know, however, that the world we work in is very diverse. Also know that diversity can bring a fractured response to decisions that fall against a person's ideology or values. Try to suspend a child for defending himself in a fight on the playground. Tell your PTA mom that her kid needs to learn how to treat people with dignity and respect. Better yet, attempt to implement involuntary drug testing in a high school district. Or my personal favorite, work with the board to save the district from financially going bankrupt by recommending that employees increase their health benefit contributions.

Know that you must do the right thing for students, but also know that the decisions you make will make some people miserable. Recognize that it will be impossible to be liked by everyone.

A mentor once reminded me that if one was to become a true leader, they needed to have *the heart of an angel and the skin of a rhino*. What a great metaphor. I used this comparison often when making decisions that were not popular. As a result, not everyone *really liked me!*

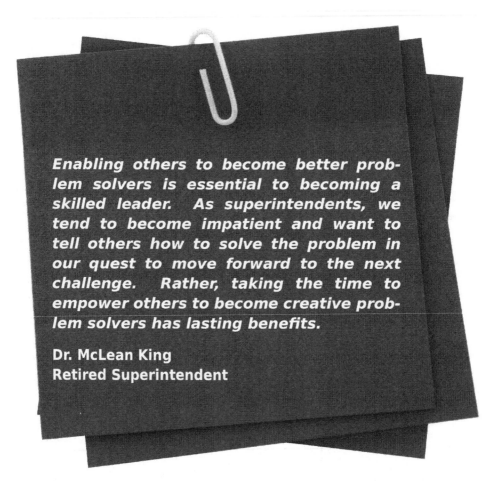

*Enabling others to become better problem solvers is essential to becoming a skilled leader. As superintendents, we tend to become impatient and want to tell others how to solve the problem in our quest to move forward to the next challenge. Rather, taking the time to empower others to become creative problem solvers has lasting benefits.*

**Dr. McLean King**
**Retired Superintendent**

# 31. CRUISE CONTROL

If you are thinking about purchasing a new car, try to do so before moving to a new district or job. Also, if you plan to take a vacation, try to keep your plans under the radar and not share the details with the people at work.

As an educational leader you will no doubt be in the higher earning bracket than most of your employees. You will be working alongside clerks, custodians, cafeteria workers and secretaries that make a fraction of your salary. While they know we make "the big bucks," it doesn't pay to flaunt it. I like to travel, but usually kept that information close to the vest since I didn't want people to think I was sipping wine overlooking the Eiffel Tower while they were trying to make ends meet, living paycheck to paycheck.

So, keep your cruises under control and purchase your BMW, Mercedes or sports cars before you move to a new district or job. Better yet, drive an ordinary car that won't call attention to your high salary. This helpful tip also can apply to diamonds, remodeling, hot tubs, boats, and other luxury items.

## 32.   CAFETERIA STYLE

As a school principal I never seemed to find time to eat a proper lunch and as a result gained a lot of unnecessary weight. When I first became a school principal I found myself snacking constantly on chocolate candy bars or potato chips in the staff room. I soon learned that the only way to keep off added pounds was to eat three meals a day; a difficult task working at a busy school.

One day I was sitting on the lunch benches talking to a few students and came up with this great idea. Why not eat lunch with my students every day? This could be a major two-for-one, I thought; a good lunch and time to actually talk with our students. This particular brainstorm was one of my best ideas ever! Throughout my seven years as a middle school principal, I ate lunch with students almost every day. It was truly one of the most rewarding and beneficial times for me. Not only was I eating a nutritious lunch, but I was able to learn more about the school, how students felt about their teachers and what they thought needed to be improved. Students became so accustomed to my lunchtime visits that many of them would begin asking early in the day if I would sit with them during lunch.

Word traveled fast; students soon learned that if they shared problems such as no toilet paper in the restrooms or disrespectful noon aides, that I would take charge and make things right. This pleasant lunchtime activity became so popular with students that it eventually evolved into Friday lunches with the principal for those students receiving Citizen of the Month or Honor Roll awards.

As a superintendent, the joy of eating lunch with students became a little more complicated, especially at the high school level. High school students made it perfectly clear they didn't want the superintendent eating lunch with them, so the next best thing for me was to seek out middle school students. This age group loves to have important people [at least in their mind] eat lunch with them and ask questions.

As I review my career as an educational leader, the most rewarding experiences I had were those moments when I ate lunch and talked informally with my students. I also remembered to check in with the cafeteria staff each day to thank them for serving a great lunch. And yes, I kept my weight down as a result of eating one lunch rather than sixteen snacks a day.

## 33.    LOOKING FOR PRAISE IN ALL THE WRONG PLACES

While it may seem that you are working hard without much in the way of recognition, be assured that those who count know how hard you work. We spend so much of our time acknowledging others in our leadership roles and rarely hear praise come our way. If you are doing your job and making good decisions for children then know this.

It is inevitable that at any given time, over half of a given constituent will be against your decision and not your biggest fan. If you are pleasing everyone, then it's safe to say you aren't leading. Positive affirmation and recognition usually come from within because people are not quick to bestow praise on us. Just know that you are making a difference for students and know that most of the people you serve appreciate and care about your dedication and hard work. If you go looking for praise, you won't find it, so don't waste your time trying.

## 34.  THE HARD TRUTH

Leadership is an expression of ourselves, and sometimes negative feedback can cut to our core and leave us feeling vulnerable. However, feedback is very necessary for the success of any leader. Feedback can help you correct small issues before they become serious problems later.

In order to get authentic feedback, you need to ask for it on a regular basis and truly demonstrate you are open to accepting it. One of the best ways to do this is to take something small and immediately implement a change based on feedback you have received. I asked for feedback from my leadership team during a full day retreat and one of the things that came out of the meeting was my response to emails. I was always on email and responded quickly to questions or problems. However, I did NOT always send a response when someone would send me information such as a grade level team meeting agenda or cc me on an email. A few of my teachers interpreted this to mean that I was being unresponsive and assumed that I did not care. I was horrified! Of course I cared! It was a very small thing that over time sent the wrong message to some of my staff. No wonder they were a bit resistant.

From that point forward, I responded to EVERY email even if it was just a simple "thank you." Had I not asked for feedback, this small issue would have continued to grow indefinitely.

## 35.  GLORY HOUND

R esearch suggests that affirming people's accomplishments at work can lead to higher employee morale and satisfaction. People want to feel validated in the workplace and as the leader you have the power and the responsibility to confirm that those who work in your organization matter, and what they do has value.

One way to accomplish this is to make people feel appreciated by sharing any credit for your own work or dedication to projects. As a superintendent I always tried to ensure that school board members were given recognition for their dedication to students and community. For example, when introducing a new program for approval that I could have publicly taken credit for, I would openly share the credit with the board by acknowledging their work on the project and for overseeing district program development. Sometimes it sounded like, "I would like to thank the board for all their time and effort spent on the technology steering committee that enabled our district to secure one million dollars in technology funds." Most people were well aware that I "deserved" the recognition, but they were equally impressed that the credit for this major project was shared with school board members.

Additionally as a school principal I made sure to acknowledge teachers who worked alongside of me on projects or initiatives. Interestingly, I learned this lesson the hard way. As principal, our school finally hit the coveted "800" API mark and became a proud member of the "800 Club" in our district. To recognize this achievement, our school received a plaque from the School Board.

So excited and proud of the school's accomplishment, I hung the plaque in my office. Several months later it was disclosed in a leadership team meeting that some teachers were offended that the plaque was displayed in my office rather than the office foyer. This oversight was quite a rookie principal faux pas.

Needless to say I rushed back to my office and personally hung the plaque in the foyer. Leadership involves building effective teams and sharing the power; no one wants their leader to "hog" the limelight.

*The core skills of a successful educational leader are the same as all leaders – build relationships through honesty and authenticity; lead with foresight and vision that inspires others; focus on personal and organizational core values; demonstrate competency in your work. Stay focused on this core, keeping in mind that service to our young people is our legacy.*

**Dr. Keith Larick**
**Retired Superintendent**
**Professor of Organizational Leadership,**
**Brandman University**

## 36. LOST IN TRANSLATION

As we know, it is important to communicate to all stakeholders in an organization. Part of that critical communication process involves providing language translations for open meetings, parent events, and important written communique.

As a new school administrator I was responsible for our school's Open House and communicating the information to parents. When it was time to write a parent letter, I was keenly aware that I needed to communicate in both English and Spanish due to our student population. I collected several samples of Open House letters over many years that I had kept in a file. Hoping to impress my new boss and be efficient, I took a sample letter, re-typed it and changed the dates. Voila! I was all done and it was off to the presses.

I have to say I was feeling pretty proud of myself for being so clever, until, one of my Spanish speaking teachers came in to my office with the letter in his hand and delicately told me that I had made a slight error. He proceeded to tell me that because I had left off the tilde (the little swirl you see above the "n" in Spanish words) on the word "año", I had actually said "anus" instead of "year." So much for being clever, I now felt like an "ano!"

Lesson learned, be careful when trying to accomplish a task too quickly, especially when translating an English message into a foreign language. While our limited English parents can be very forgiving with our attempts at communicating in their language, know that things can get lost in translation and make us look bad to our public!

## 37.   YOU'VE GOT MAIL

A s an educational leader you will soon learn that everyone wants access to your time. At first you won't mind the Sunday evening phone call, 5 a.m. text message or responding to a panicked email at 1:00 in the morning.

However, after keeping up with the 24/7 demands of non-stop communication, you will most likely find yourself exhausted and your family ready to cry mutiny. As you continue to reinforce this habit, more and more people will expect you to be available and responsive around the clock.

There is only one person who can help set appropriate boundaries and that is YOU! As a leader, some contact is unavoidable outside of normal working hours, but only you can set the limits for what that will look like. If these limits are not defined, you will forever be a slave to your iPhone, Blackberry or email. Most importantly, this is not healthy over the long run and sends an unspoken message to your followers that you expect the same from them in return.

If you tell your followers you believe family comes first and work and life balance is important, you must be prepared to model it. I still do NOT have work email forwarded to my personal phone and will continue to uphold this boundary. If I need to access my work email, it can be accomplished via the web. You are the one in control. Because, let's face it, email is inevitable.

## 38.    GOOGLE THIS

Hosting a blog, personal web site, or an account on a social networking site can impact your career and job search, for better or for worse. I recently read a blog in which the creator wrote he lies in interviews. That certainly would not thrill a prospective or current employer if they knew about it. Another job seeker's blog mentions that she loves to party all night, drinks to excess on a regular basis, hates her boss, and steals office supplies on occasion. Again, this is not a profile that would excite most employers.

Be aware that your current and prospective employers are taking time to read your Facebook posts and are checking in on your personal web sites and/or blogs as well.

There is no doubt that social media plays a very important and sometimes dangerous role in our society. With the advent of Facebook, Twitter, LinkedIn almost everyone is online. You need to decide early on what your policy will be when it comes to social media. Will you take friend requests from current employees, past employees, peers and your boss? Will you have a personal page AND a professional page?

I developed a policy that involved not having current employees on my personal Facebook page. As friend requests from staff came in, I simply informed them of my policy. In this way I was able to make sure it did not come across as personal. Having even one staff member as a friend but not accepting the request of another can be deadly.

The internet is a wonderful thing; however, it creates a permanent record of you. As important as it is to manage employees and an organization, it is also important to manage your digital footprint and online identity. Nowadays, one of the first things people do is to Google your name. I have been Googled prior to attending interviews, after newspapers reported my hiring, and currently by students taking my course as a professor. Your digital footprint is often your first impression with many stakeholders. Every so often, Google yourself to find out what is online about you. Websites such as ratemyteacher.com also include school administrator ratings that can be complimentary as well as damaging.

If you find something derogatory or false on the internet about you, contact the website host for removal. There are also companies that can assist you in removing negative or false content and several services that can enhance your status or branding on the web.

As mentioned, it's now common practice for employers to Google people they are interested in hiring. If your personal website address is listed on your resume, make sure it deals with your professional career and not personal information. One hiring manager shared that he always reviews an applicant's web site if listed. Another reported that she would try to find out as much about a candidate as possible, including searching the person online.

Here are some Facebook, web site, and blog Do's and Don'ts:

- Don't include a link on your resume to any site which includes content that is not appropriate for a business audience.

- Be very careful what you put online. If you have a MySpace or Facebook account, people you don't want to read your profile may be able to access it, even if you think nobody will read it. Make your account private, so only your friends can access it. Be extra careful and don't post anything that you don't want a prospective employer to read.

- Be mindful of what you write. Just about anything that is online can be read by someone - or everyone. If you don't want the world to read what you've posted, make sure they can't.

- Blogging and using Facebook can become a passion, so don't let that passion hinder your employment prospects. Keep blogging and communicating through Facebook but blog safely, securely and carefully so your career opportunities aren't jeopardized.

# 39.   WIN THE WAR, NOT THE BATTLE

At times, being an educational leader can feel like you are walking through a never ending minefield. Parent complaints, bad press reports, angry board members, contract issues, the list is endless. Avoid your natural instinct to win every battle that comes your way. Most battles carry political costs and benefits. Sometimes winning the war means strategically losing some of the battles along the way.

For example, leaders need to look at the big picture from the mountaintop to analyze strategy. If yielding to one angry teacher or parent means he or she will gain some recognition and power, so be it; you know over the long run, the win is not that important. It is the big picture that is important; let it go.

A colleague once shared that the school district he was leading had a long history of antagonistic relations with the local municipality. Neither entity trusted the other at all. The Redevelopment Tax Increment gave both the city and the district an opportunity to acquire funds for badly needed improvements but, since the city was the lead agency for this matter, the district could not benefit without the city taking action. Prior to this man becoming superintendent, the district had publicly criticized the city for its lack of action and planning. This, predictably, did not improve relations or spur the city to action, even though the city stood to benefit greatly.

Since the district needed the redevelopment funds for a variety of improvements, including a new central facility, a strategy was needed to get the city to act. However, the City Council and its staff were defensive about the growing reputation of the district as an aggressive and progressive organization and the public perception of the city as backward. In addition, it was discovered during staff level discussions that the city's staff did not fully understand the mechanics of redevelopment. As surprising as this was, it presented an opportunity. The city needed an opportunity to show itself as progressive; properly presented, redevelopment offered that opportunity. The district just wanted the money.

The district did a complete analysis of the redevelopment situation, highlighting benefits to the city, packaged it and gave it to the City Finance Director to present as her idea. She took it to the City Manager, who wanted to look good, and he took it to the City Council, who desperately wanted to look good in the public's eye. The City Council then took action to approve an extension and amendments to the Redevelopment Agency and took full credit for the actions and the plan as well as the benefits the district was to receive. The district got no credit for the plan; it just got the money, which was really the win.

Fighting the city would never have moved it to action. Giving them an opportunity to save face did. The current District Central Facility is magnificent and is a testimony to the wisdom of winning, not fighting.

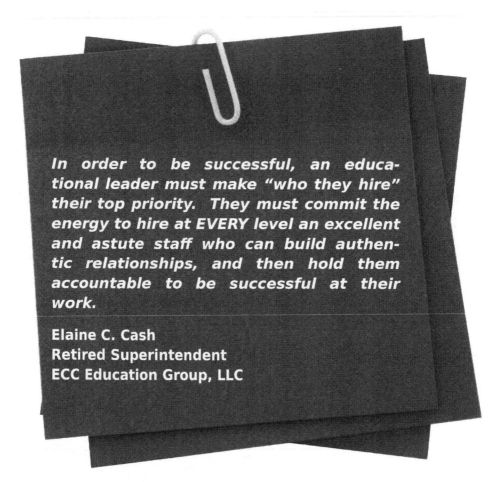

*In order to be successful, an educational leader must make "who they hire" their top priority.  They must commit the energy to hire at EVERY level an excellent and astute staff who can build authentic relationships, and then hold them accountable to be successful at their work.*

**Elaine C. Cash**
**Retired Superintendent**
**ECC Education Group, LLC**

# 40.  ROLL CALL

B e prepared to attend the funerals of your employees. Also prepare to attend the funerals of your employees' spouses and children. In 30 years serving as an educational leader I only missed one funeral; that of a principal's husband. To the best of my knowledge no one ever commented on the funerals I attended, only the one I missed.

Also, it is respectful to have a district or school policy that involves sending out a hand written letter to the family, signed by the superintendent/principal to express condolences. At the site, it is appropriate to ensure that floral arrangements and donations are sent to families during times of mourning.

Effective leaders must ensure that during periods of sadness and grief employees are recognized and supported by their workplace families.

## 41.  SMALL WORLD AFTER ALL

The world of educational administration is surprisingly small. Before you know, you will feel as if you are in the middle of a *Six Degrees of Kevin Bacon* game. This game is based on the "six degrees of separation" theory, which states everyone is a mere six or fewer acquaintance links apart.

This theory could not be truer than in the world of educational administration. People who work in our field, especially school districts, are very well connected. The pipeline is fluid, and news travels fast. If you badmouth a current employer or coworker, that information travels fast and may hurt your reputation or any chances for promotion. It's a small world and it's important to maintain your professionalism and not put your career in jeopardy.

One night, I received a disturbing phone call from my friend, a school superintendent. We taught together in one school district and later worked as principals in another district. My friend wanted me to know that he overheard his district custodian telling a secretary that someone on my cabinet was criticizing the superintendent [that's me]. Small world.

On another occasion, I recently presented information to a room of over 250 doctoral students and adjunct faculty. Looking around, I took note that the room was filled with many people I had previously worked with while going through my own doctoral program. Upon second glance I noticed that many of these folks also worked as administrators with me in several districts prior to becoming a fulltime faculty member at the University. As Co-Chair of the doctoral program, I personally hired many of our adjunct faculty in the room. Some of these adjuncts included an assistant superintendent, a director of staff development, and an elementary curriculum director, all who worked with me during my first year as a school principal.

Most notably, my former doctoral dissertation chair was in the room. He later became my boss when he hired me to serve as a principal in his district. Then after moving to the university level, I had the opportunity to hire him as one of our adjunct professors. *I was now technically HIS BOSS!* It's a very small world after all.

## 42.    TO TELL THE TRUTH

Take note: as a leader, don't lie, stretch the truth, or say "no" when you know the answer is "yes." If someone asks you a question that you clearly do not want to answer, there are various ways to skirt the issue. For example, if someone asks you, "Was it true that a student had a gun on campus?" You can always respond by saying, "I am not at liberty to answer this question right now as we are still investigating." If someone manages to gets you in a corner, make sure you have an available escape hatch up your sleeve so that you don't get caught in a lie. We all know what happened to President Clinton and his perceived loss of credibility. *Don't lie... never lie... thou shall not tell a lie.*

To avoid lying to your stakeholders and lesson the probability of losing points with your followers try using some of the following tactics when confronted with a question you don't want to answer:

### 1. Respond to a question with a question
If someone asks if there was a gun on campus, respond back with your own question with something like "How did you hear that? Tell me more?" Act professional and maintain an even tone in an attempt to throw the focus back on the other person rather than you.

### 2. Change the subject
While this tactic is not always successful, it does provide the opportunity to move the subject of the conversation away from the original topic. For example, if someone asks you if you are mad at the new assistant superintendent you might want to interject with something like, "Did you happen to receive that email I sent to everyone

last night about joining the Educational Foundation?" This immediate change in the original subject leaves people thinking you're not going to answer and even may help them forget what they were asking in the first place.

### 3. Laugh it off

This strategy may come with a bit of your own personal sarcasm but can work effectively to derail an immediate response out of you. Laughing at a question asked or rolling your eyes upward saying, "Sure, or wouldn't you like to know," always works when you don't want to divulge the truth or get caught in a lie.

### 4. Act stupid

Sounds like a stupid strategy, but this works wonders to keep yourself from not telling the truth. Such phrases as "Really? No Way." or "How silly of them," are great tactics to keep an incorrect answer from flying out of your mouth.

### 5. Just Walk Away

Finally, my preferred method, is to say that you have an important meeting you must attend, and that you will get back to them; anything but to give an immediate response.

One last thought about not telling the truth. There is a fine line between exaggeration and lying. Don't confuse the two. As educators we are often prone to exaggeration. Embellished stories are more a sign of a creative imagination than of a person who does not tell the truth. Remember, there is small distinction between the two, so be careful how much you exaggerate when making a point or being asked a targeted question. We all know the most serious setback for a leader is to be accused of telling a lie. Take note of the celebrated words of Nietzsche, *"I'm not upset that you lied to me, I'm upset that from now on I can't believe you."*

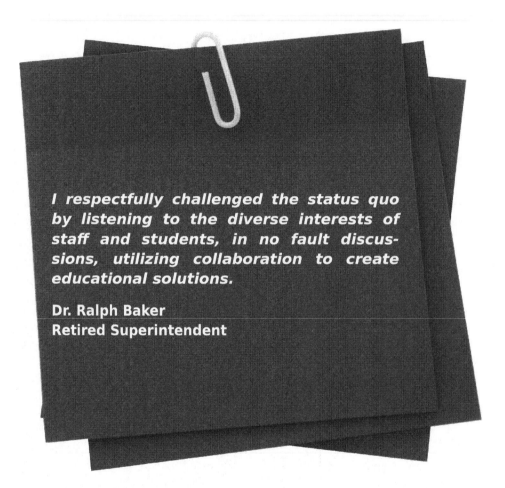

*I respectfully challenged the status quo by listening to the diverse interests of staff and students, in no fault discussions, utilizing collaboration to create educational solutions.*

**Dr. Ralph Baker**
**Retired Superintendent**

## 43. DEATH BY MEETING

T ime is a precious commodity in educational administration. Despite this, my calendar seemed to always be riddled with a never-ending stream of meetings. Leadership meetings, curriculum meetings, Board meetings, parent meetings, and staff meetings seemed to rule my life.

One deadly mistake as a leader is to bore your staff to death with meetings; everyone is just as busy as you are. A main rule I always followed was, if I could provide the information in a memo of some sort I would. I called these, "Staff Meetings on Paper." If collaboration of some sort was required, I would hold the meeting in person.

The gift of time is one of the greatest gifts you can bestow on a busy professional. Staff knew that I valued their time and if a face-to-face meeting was required they knew it was going to be important. Not only was I respected for valuing their time, but the number of teachers arriving late or grading papers throughout the meeting decreased as a result of only hosting meetings that required full collaboration and staff input.

So the next time you are in a leadership meeting, look around the room. If everyone looks as if they have lost the will to live, consider hosting your next meeting in a memo.

# 44.  NO PARKING

The subject of reserved parking spots is loaded with controversy. The only perk I ever wanted as a school leader was
a designated parking space. As a principal, I wanted that space
even more. The problem with taking advantage of the special
parking space is that people are inclined to think you believe you
are superior to them.

When arriving to a new district or assignment, if no allocated
parking space exists, don't request one or you will be asking for
trouble. If you arrive at a new job and see a parking space designated "Principal" or "Superintendent" think twice before assuming the parking space.

In one district, I had the parking sign painted over and
received overwhelming admiration from everyone. Besides, do
you really want employees or students [who may be angry with
your latest decision] to know where your car is located? I know of
many administrators with slashed tires and keyed paint.

## 45.   GO TO THE HEAD OF THE CLASS

A s a school principal and school superintendent, I set a goal to substitute teach in a classroom each year. I volunteered for this assignment once a year since it afforded me the opportunity to remember what it was like to serve as a classroom teacher.

As a principal, I substituted for an eighth grade English language teacher and found it extremely difficult, even though I spent an entire weekend prepping for the assignment. Throughout the day, I began to realize how very difficult the job of a teacher is, especially those charged with teaching English language learners or special needs students. My yearly substitute teaching exposure caused almost everyone in the school community, including PTA parents, to think my dedication to the profession was admirable, if not courageous. Our students got the biggest kick out of seeing me in their classroom, but more importantly I gained respect from the teachers because I was willing *to* walk in their shoes for a day.

As a superintendent, it became a lot more difficult to gain access to a substitute gig. It seemed, for some reason, that teachers were very fearful of the superintendent taking over their classroom for the day. One year I lucked out when the union president announced he was attending a conference and needed approval for a substitute teacher. I requested to be his substitute teacher for the day and he responded with a resounding yes. Upon my offer to substitute, he could not contain his delight and had a Cheshire cat grin on his face. He was ecstatic; the top leader would be teaching his four high school political science classes.

In response to his excitement, I dug further; all of his classes were overflowing with 42-45 students, a result of budget cuts and increased class size. He couldn't wait for me to share his pain. Well pain I got. I would like to personally go on record to state that teaching in his classroom was probably one the roughest days ever of my career EVER! I could barely stand up at the end of the day and almost had to miss the following day of work as a result of extreme fatigue. I was also mortified that I had to call the school principal (on my cell phone) to help me with some uncontrollable students, which proved to be rather humorous when school employees heard about the incident. In spite of all the problems, I ended up feeling very satisfied about spending this valuable time in the classroom.

As a result of these experiences, I was able to make better decisions as a superintendent, knowing exactly what high school teachers were held responsible for each day. Not only did volunteering to substitute reap huge leadership points from the rank-and-file, but the experience actually served as a filter for decisions made later involving high school concerns.

The first action I took the following week was to leverage my substitute stint with the Board of Education to entertain the possibility of lowering class size. What were we thinking, 45 students to a classroom? How quickly we forget how difficult a teacher's job really is. Attending to so many students on an hourly basis for content knowledge, lesson design, student engagement and classroom management, if done properly, is quite an art form. As a leader, if you want to show your teachers you care about them as professionals and equally enhance your instructional decision making filter, volunteer to substitute teach for one day each year. Once you recover, you will be glad you did.

---

Excerpts from "Go to the Head of the Class"
*The School Administrator*, October 2009

## 46. HELP IS ON THE WAY

Having worked in many school districts, I quickly discovered that the majority of site administrators or teachers were not particularly avid fans of district office staff.

District office people tend to bring new ideas and programs to schools, which have a way of causing more work and stress for those working in the classroom. When teachers push back, district staff can be heard saying, "We're just here to help, so let us know what we can do to support you." The "we're here to help" slogan is widely used in districts and most site people are familiar with the phrase.

As a newly appointed assistant superintendent of educational services, I was cautious to avoid using this slogan with its negative connotations. I found this task difficult and caught myself several times in mid-sentence, "I'm just here to..." To counteract this negative perception, I visited sites daily, asked questions, and worked with teachers to get them the tools they needed to be successful. I worked hard to gain their trust and respect, rather than to force my programs into their classrooms. We worked together as a team to realize district goals.

So remember that when you show up at a site or in a teacher's classroom, try to avoid the "we're here to help" hot button.

*Educational leaders understand that leadership is more than being well liked. Leadership means strength of character which means making tough decisions and doing things not because they are popular but because it is the right thing to do. Do the right thing no matter how attractive or profitable the wrong thing may be.*

**Chief Moitoso**
**Retired School Board Member**

## 47.   TRIGGER HAPPY

A s a school administrator I never hesitated to call 911 in an emergency, especially when it involved a student or employee.

I vividly recall two 911 situations; one involving an eighth grader lying motionless on the playground during recess and the second, a follow- up call from the superintendent suggesting I was 911 trigger happy. The student sprawled out on the ground, head flopped to one side was notorious for pranks, but this time something didn't seem right; his face was pale gray. While I knew there was a good chance he may be faking it, I didn't want to take a chance with his life, or my career for that matter, so I radioed the secretary, directing her to call 911. After 911 was contacted, I was convinced the right decision had been made; this child was not faking. The paramedics arrived and discovered the student had been knocked out; no bones broken, but a recommendation was made to transport the student to the local emergency room for observation.

Later in the day, the phone call came from the superintendent reminding me that I needed to be more cautious when calling 911 as these services, he reprimanded, "Don't come cheap." During the time I worked in this district I chose to ignore his scolding and continued to call 911 for every student believed injured and not able to stand up or [God forbid] passed out on the ground.

Just recently I spotted an article in a local paper reporting that a school principal had been encouraged to publically apologize for not authorizing her staff to dial 911 after a first grade student injured himself on campus. The school principal made her apology as directed in front of at least 30 parents and a handful of staff during a meeting at the school. "I am not here to add to a parent's anguish when a child is injured," she told audience members. "I don't ever want to hurt a child or cause distress." Apparently the student had stumbled into the school's front office with blood coming from his forehead after he fell on the playground. Office staff immediately began to dial 911, but the principal advised them to call his mother instead. "I was focused on getting his mom here first, and I don't know why," the principal reported. The child's mother ended up calling 911 herself after coming to the school. She later said her son missed two days of classes as a result of a concussion.

Cardinal Rule: Don't hesitate to call 911 in the event of an emergency. Act quickly and worry about repercussions later!

# 48. DOG TIRED

Most teachers believe school administration is a life threatening position, but I doubt many administrators think the same thing about teaching. Here's the real story and I share this opinion openly. As a former teacher, I ended my day planning for the next day's lessons, clearing off my desk, cleaning up the classroom, and stopping by the main office to pick up messages. Before going home, I would sit in my car for a few minutes before starting the engine. I needed to catch my breath; I was exhausted. Teaching six different lessons of math and science to students who needed me to be "on" every second took an incredible amount of energy. While I knew I wanted to be an administrator, I started to doubt myself. How could I work any longer? These administrators have killer hours.

As an administrator I did work longer hours, there was no doubt about that. But the hours were unlike a teacher's workday that was concentrated with little time to breathe. Administrator hours are spread out over the day. By that I mean I could use the restroom whenever I wanted (big perk), could catch a cup of coffee or make a telephone call.

It didn't take me long to learn that my job overseeing hundreds of students during and after school as an assistant principal was unlike that of a teacher who was always accountable to a set group of students and confined to a classroom. As a principal I would walk through classrooms every day, supervise lunch and monitor the passing of classes; all good exercise in my opinion. At the end of the day, I was tired, but not the "drop dead" fatigue I experienced as a teacher.

This is not a fact often shared by administrators but it is the truth. Working as a school administrator is stressful and has long hours, but the job is not as physically or mentally exhausting as teaching in a classroom, constantly having to "be on" for every student. The job of an administrator is exciting and has a sense of freedom that enables one to withstand some of the job stress.

As an educational leader it is important that we *never forget* how exhausted our teachers are at the end of the day. More importantly, try to remember this important concept when asking them to take on one more committee, task force or extra assignment.

# 49. THE PARENT TRAP

I held a parent conference with a very angry man one day. He could hardly contain his contempt for our school. "I know my daughter did something wrong," he stated, "but the teacher humiliated her in class. I want this man fired and brought up on child abuse charges." After spending a considerable amount of time listening to this parent's complaints, I learned that the teacher caught the student putting on lip gloss during class. The teacher then went over to the student, grabbed the lip gloss and proceeded to go outside the portable classroom and throw the lip gloss on the roof. End of story. Bad story. One hour later, I was able to persuade this teacher to apologize to both the student and parent.

When holding a meeting with an upset parent and student of any age, first try to talk to the parent alone without the child. This strategy allows the parent to vent without the child being forced to choose between the authority of the home and the authority of the school. Attempt to work with the parent to agree that "we are both supporting the child."

When working with a parent, some ideas to reflect upon when mediating a conflict include:

**1. Separate people from the problem by trying to identify the problem.**

Ask yourself, why is this person here? What is the problem? If you can find out what you are actually dealing with, you won't get sidetracked with other concerns. For example, a lot of parents come into a conference hating the whole school system when really they are mad at a custodian who treated their child badly. Get to the heart of the problem by asking probing questions.

### 2. Put yourself in their shoes.

Imagine that you are a single mom, or a parent of a special needs child who thinks the school's job is to help their child at all costs. Try to envision yourself in that person's shoes and imagine the problem from their end. Sometimes this is really hard to do, depending on the "various type of shoes" but once you get the hang of it, it's a miracle problem solving strategy. For example I have never experienced poverty first hand, and as a leader it was initially very difficult for me to envision what it must be like to be truly poor. But I know how to imagine. I knew that in order for me to help those who live in poverty that I had to first imagine what it must be like to be poor. I had to envision what it would be like to purchase food and clothing for a family with little or no money, to have no transportation, to stand in endless lines at social services or not have money for your child's yearbook. As a result I could imagine how difficult it must be for a poor mother, coming into my office, angry about the notice she received saying her child can't graduate unless she comes up with a $65 textbook fine. Take the time to get into their shoes.

### 3. Deal with emotion first, substance second.

Ask probing questions to reduce the tension in the room and engender empathy. Work on getting the negative or hostile tone out of the room. I was always fairly successful at toning down angry mothers; I'd touch their shoulder or try to make some womanly connection. Angry dads, however, were another story. Allowing them time to vent was usually the best strategy. Once they got the anger out of their system we could begin to deal with the actual problem.

### 4. Ask, "What would you like to see happen?"

These words served as my *silver bullet* throughout my career. I never tried to resolve any conflict without first uttering this phrase. Yes, Mr. Angry Dad, *what would you like to see happen* here? Do you want the bully who hit your son suspended? Do you want your son's teacher reprimanded or fired or could it be as simple as... *Do you want an apology?*

### 5. Guide, don't decide.

Sounds like a platitude, but it's a good one. Help your parents and students figure out the answers to their own problems. Guide them to logical solutions. Help them make up their own resolutions; don't tell them how it's going to go down but rather ask them what strategies they plan to employ to solve their problem.

### 6. And finally, help all parties leave every interaction with grace and not regret.

You can do it, just follow the above recommendations, learn to listen, get into their shoes, work to lower the anger in the room, and ask those 7 magic words.

# 50.  SHARE THE WEALTH

As a leader, whenever I became involved with an agonizing problem, the kind that would wake me up in the middle of the night in a cold sweat thinking, *what am I going to do?* I would lean on an important leadership concept to alleviate the fear.

I learned from my mentors that by sharing the problem with concerned stakeholders I could spread out of the effects of the problem. I knew that it was critical to bring certain people that were affected by the problem into the fold so the burden wouldn't be shouldered by one individual.

I'm not referring to decisions leaders are hired to make on their own. Rather, I'm talking about a major district problem, a problem that one person should not have to assume responsibility for by themselves. For example, when I first learned that a teacher had sent an offensive, racist email joke to several of her colleagues within the district, I immediately got on the phone to apprise our Board President. Upon first hearing the news, she was relentless, chastising the district for not having established email protocols. But I knew my instinct to share the problem with her was a good one. I knew that she and I would eventually work on a solution we could both live with. This situation had the potential to blow up in the media and I recognized her help was required to navigate the crisis.

School principals, however, often have a difficult time with this thinking in that they believe they are charged with making every decision. Somehow they get it in their minds that sharing bad news with the superintendent will only cause trouble and perhaps they might be accused of not running their schools properly. As a superintendent I continually reminded our principals that it was important to share any problems so we could strategize the best possible solutions.

I first became familiar with this *share the wealth* tactic during my first year as middle school principal. One afternoon, right before dismissal, my assistant principal discovered that a student was carrying a loaded gun on campus. By five o'clock that evening, news had traveled fast and the community was in an uproar. The media magically appeared on our school's doorstep in an attempt to interview me. While a loaded gun wasn't something one would keep from the superintendent, I knew I would need his support to survive this crisis.

The next day he showed up in the front office holding two cups of coffee, one in each hand. He handed me one of the cups and as we walked into my office he said, "I'm here for the day, I'm yours. Together we will get through this problem." I'll never forget that gesture; it was important to know that the top person in the district cared enough to guide me through a very serious challenge as a leader.

Later, after becoming a superintendent, whenever I learned that one of our administrators was facing a similar situation, I made sure to arrive at the school early in the morning, holding two cups of coffee. No matter what side of the fence you sit on, make sure that you don't shoulder major crises alone and remember to extend positive support when someone on your leadership team needs help during a difficult time.

# 51. ANGER MANAGEMENT

I read recently the following aphorism: Fear is not a workplace motivator. I suspect many of us have had the sad occasion at one time or another to work for someone who was just plain mean. So mean that they took out all their insecurities and anger on their employees. If things went wrong for them, watch out.

I am hoping that if you are reading this book, you are not one of those mean and angry leaders, as you will not need the tips in this book for long. Treating employees with disrespect, calling them names, yelling or demeaning them at work is not high on the leadership Richter scale. In fact, employees in the modern age know they do not have to tolerate a bully boss and have learned how to file hostile work environment charges. If your anger is generated from insecurity, keep it to yourself. Work with a mentor or professional to discuss why you are angry and what you can do to overcome your insecurity.

It's no secret that employees don't like to be yelled at. A leader prone to angry outbursts risks the relationship between boss and employee, which can lead to an overall breakdown in organizational effectiveness. Exhibiting too much anger is probably the number one reason why leaders fail. Employees learn to keep away from an angry boss.

I remember working alongside an HR director who would exhibit flashes of anger within a split second. People would come to my desk before going into her office and ask, "What kind of a mood is she in today?" No one wanted to say anything to this woman for fear she would explode. Within two years she was fired; everyone was afraid of her.

If you have anger issues, get them under control by seeking to determine their root causes. Work to understand the importance of anger management in the workplace and learn to express all of your emotions appropriately. If you don't manage this undesirable trait, don't expect to serve in a leadership position for long.

So if you are an angry leader, is all lost? No, you can be an effective leader if you are willing to practice anger management strategies and show concern for how your anger affects others.

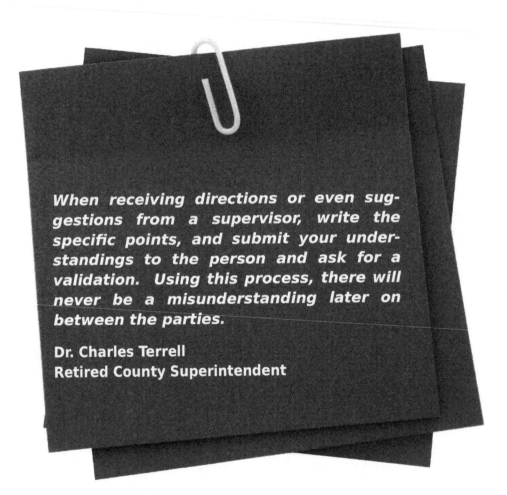

When receiving directions or even suggestions from a supervisor, write the specific points, and submit your understandings to the person and ask for a validation. Using this process, there will never be a misunderstanding later on between the parties.

Dr. Charles Terrell
Retired County Superintendent

## 52.   RUN A MILE IN MY SHOES!

On a middle school campus, one of the things you learn quickly is a strong physical education department usually cuts down on school-wide discipline. It is also likely to be the department you visit the least if it is running smoothly with little or no problems.

With the emphasis on high visibility in classrooms, making it out to watch PE does not happen often, as it is not a high priority. One of the ways I made sure to show my support for my PE teachers was to wear PE clothes and run the mile with students on occasion. This simple act turned out to be very powerful. Students enjoyed trying to outrun me, and as a result the PE teachers felt supported. I forever had their loyalty. I would have never expected a mile could go such a long way!

As a superintendent, I was involved in a student initiative that aimed to increase student daily attendance. Well known throughout the district as a "hands-on" superintendent, I had the grand idea to take the place of an absent student and follow her schedule. My ultimate goal was to report out to the community, via the media who were following the story, exactly what instruction the student had missed in one day. The news media was excited; they believed my stint would make an interesting educational story: *Superintendent Takes Student's Seat*. Little did I know that this "seat" involved running a mile.

As luck had it, PE was the first class on this student's schedule and the weather was freezing, not uncommon to the Central Valley in early November. The PE teachers were prepared; they arranged for me to wear some actual student PE clothing. I was happy to accommodate, but due to the cold weather, I left on my black opaque tights under the gym shorts. Running a mile was easy for me since I run daily; it was fun and exhilarating. Three news channels and one newspaper photo editor followed me around the track as I ran my mile. I was really lovin' the attention; I felt really important; so much media attention. The next morning, my assistant principal texted me with the following update: "New fashion statement in the Bee." I ran out of the house, picked up the newspaper on the driveway and gasped. A full color, front page image exposed me running around the track in gym shorts with black tights. This photo still mortifies me to this day. *Run a mile in my shoes; run a mile in black tights.*

Lesson learned; continue to be creative in an attempt to gain recognition for your initiatives, but don't get too caught up with yourself; it will surely come back to bite you.

## 53. STANDING INVITATION

As mentioned earlier in this book, visibility is crucial if you are a site administrator, but this is only half of the equation. In addition to being visible before and after school, at break, lunch, or while attending sporting events or school plays, visiting classrooms is one of the most important tasks you will ever engage in as a leader.

Whether you are a principal, district chief academic officer or superintendent, classrooms are where the magic happens and visiting them shows everyone how much you care. Teachers work tirelessly to plan engaging lessons for their students. So often I hear, "My principal NEVER visits my classroom," or "I only saw my principal twice all year, and just for one minute." You want to be sure that is never said about you!

As the instructional leader, a large portion of your day should be focused on instruction. Being in classrooms pays big dividends such as increased accountability, decreases in student discipline, improved instructional practices, and improved teacher motivation.

When visiting classrooms, teachers want to hear from you. Leave a quick hand-written note or send an email or text on the spot! In addition to acknowledging teachers privately, I would often follow up classroom visitations with an email to my entire staff highlighting some of the great things I observed. As a superintendent, after visiting a school I always sent out a congratulatory email to the entire staff for a job well done in meeting the needs of our students.

Do not leave this part of your day to chance; it should not be an afterthought. Schedule classroom visits into your day if you are at the site and at least once a week if you work at the district office.

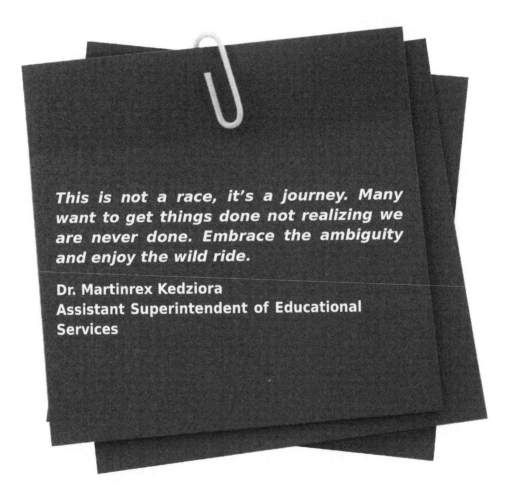

This is not a race, it's a journey. Many want to get things done not realizing we are never done. Embrace the ambiguity and enjoy the wild ride.

Dr. Martinrex Kedziora
Assistant Superintendent of Educational Services

## 54.  WHAT'S COOKING

People in organizations like to know what's going on. That's called communication! One method that helped me to become a better communicator as a leader was my regular Friday reports.

As a principal and superintendent I always wrote a Friday report called *What's Cooking* that included some information to apprise people of the accomplishments of the week or report on items everyone needed to know. The report wasn't lengthy but it needed to recap the entire week. I also used this forum to acknowledge good work and help people feel connected to the organization. This important communication vehicle became my signature trademark throughout the school district with employees and everyone looked forward to reading it each week. I used this opportunity as a way to share information with everyone in the school district.

As a result of this ongoing weekly communique I received high points for transparent communication from staff and was able to maintain honest and open communication at all levels. While a bit time-consuming to be strapped to a deliberate and ongoing project, the results are well worth the effort in that they increase your authenticity as a leader and project a culture of transparency.

# 55.    THE TEAM ROSTER

B uilding effective teams is crucial to your success as a leader. You are not a one-man band, and if you try to be one you will certainly doom yourself to failure. The people you surround yourself with will determine the extent of your success as a leader and ultimately that of the organization.

Knowing yourself is the first step. What are your strengths and weaknesses? Every team will have certain roles that need to be filled. High performing teams try to include a combination of roles such as a creative, communicator, implementer, techie, visionary, pragmatist, strategist, and facilitator. Although we are often naturally drawn to people like ourselves, you will want people on your team who will challenge your ideas and tell you the truth. Matching individuals to the needs of the team based on strengths that complement each other is crucial. Make sure you have people on your team who can compensate for your weaknesses and play off their strengths at every opportunity.

Once you have decided upon your team roster, the real work begins. Building an effective team does not happen by chance. As the leader, you will need to have a plan and be deliberate in your actions. Set the stage for high levels of trust between you and each team member and between team members on day one. Spend time building relationships. This can be achieved through one-on-one conversations with each team member and team building exercises with your entire team.

As a principal, I conducted team builders at every leadership meeting and trained my leadership teams on the principles of a Professional Learning Community. I requested they conduct team builders in their curriculum meetings. At first, it was met with some resistance; they did not see the value in it. After a few months, I had some teams actually purchase books on team building so they could conduct a new activity at each meeting. These positive interactions went a long way to build trust and a common ground to build upon.

Next, decide on a set of operating norms. This step is also often overlooked and teams pay the price later on. In the early stages of team development, the "honeymoon stage," it can be hard to imagine conflict occurring. Norms will not only help prevent unnecessary misunderstandings but help the team deal with conflict effectively when it does (and it will) occur. Norms should address and/or provide:

- A clear team structure
- Accountability expectations
- A clear decision making process
- Standardized communication structures

# 56.   GUARDIAN ANGEL

It's lonely at the top. Over time we learn who to trust and who we cannot. Most of all, we keep a keen eye on the ball and know that we work in a political arena. There will be times when your assistant principal wants your job and criticizes you in public. Or your assistant superintendent, who applied for your position and lost out, can't stand to be in the same room with you. This is when it pays to have someone in the rank and file as a trusted friend.

In every leadership position I ever assumed, I had one or two guardian angels. I didn't think much about who they were; they usually surfaced within the first month on the job. I could feel it in my gut that these people could be trusted, they liked me, and wanted me to succeed. The requirements for bonding were difficult to describe, but once the connection was made, I would nurture the relationship.

As a middle school principal his name was Bert. He was a retired Navy guy and served as the eighth grade social science teacher. His nickname was Mr. Chips. Students would follow him anywhere and do whatever he said. He was a really nice guy. I knew he was going to be my guardian angel the day I met him. He said he would do anything to help me be successful and for some reason, I believed him. He shared information that only a teacher would have; that one of his colleagues had come to work drunk, alerting me to the fact that I needed to get down to room 25 as soon as possible to take care of the situation before students arrived. He shared that a fellow teacher was planning to undermine one of my major programs and gave me some insight as to how to avoid the conflict.

While some might think this man was a traitor to his colleagues, he was not. His advisories always helped to keep an employee out of trouble, protect a student, or in the case of the alcoholic, get help rather than lose his job. In response, I was able to proactively solve problems that could have spun into major disasters.

As a superintendent, my guardian angel was actually a teacher's union official. The day we met, she said she would do anything to help me be successful and again, I believed her. She saved my job during the first year. My assistant superintendent was planning to go against a key decision of mine by siding with a board member. My guardian angel reported back to me that she heard him stating that he was going to "bury that woman." As a result of her warning I was able to get in front of a political disaster by talking with him later about the board member. I did not reveal that I knew he wanted to bury me. That would have connected his comment to my guardian angel. Knowing that I had someone on my leadership team wanting to undermine my agenda was a valuable piece of information to leverage.

So, take note of this important tip and remember to be on the lookout for your guardian angels. You'll recognize them the minute you meet.

# 57.   LOOKING GOOD

As a leader there is one cardinal rule: always try to make your boss look good! So you ask, how does one go about making the boss look good when it's all you can do to make yourself look good?

Begin by asking what you think your boss needs from you to be successful. No matter what role assumed in education, we all have bosses we report to. But remember if you are in a support role, it's important to help your bosses look like they know what they are doing at all times.

For example, when I was assistant superintendent, I never took the credit for things I knew could potentially help the superintendent stay in good favor with the board or employee unions. And, I never tried to show any of my superintendents up in public. If they were caught flat-footed without an answer to a high profile question, I made sure that somehow they got the information needed. I would say something like, "Yes, Mr. Superintendent, as you recall we scheduled a meeting to discuss the employee health benefit premium increases." While he didn't know one thing about the scheduled meeting, it didn't matter; I saved his butt in public and for that he was grateful.

Even if you think your boss is a jerk, don't go there. This is important: SUPPORT YOUR BOSS. As a superintendent I used these same tactics to make the Board look good. I always kept them informed and shared district accomplishments with them on a regular basis. I would praise them in public for supporting district initiatives, attending functions, and donating their time to the district. When you make your bosses look good, you look good in their eyes. These points can pay dividends since a boss often has control over your next career move and will remember your loyalty.

## 58. THE SLUSH FILE

Throughout my career as a school leader, I realized that the amount of daily paperwork crossing my desk was overwhelming. Even with email, the amount of paperwork piling up each week never seemed to decrease. I was frustrated that I had to sort through these huge piles of snail mail each day and just the thought of having to strain my brain over what to do with this stuff was frustrating. "Would I need this information later? If I threw this piece out would I need it three weeks from now?"

Over time, I learned to develop a personal strategy for dealing with the confusion: *paperwork rules.* Administrators are known for making up a lot of rules, and by all accounts this rule was a good one. Before attending to any of the paperwork, I promised myself that I would only touch each piece of paper once. That is, I would force myself to decide on the spot what to do with the paper while it was still in my hand. Most of the time there were four main choices:

- Choice #1 involved throwing the paperwork into the wastebasket immediately after reading. This usually involved an advertisement or a note that could be read and its contents remembered.

- Choice #2 centered on an immediate "react and respond" scenario; for example a notice detailing the date for the next Superintendent meeting or a reminder for an upcoming PTA event. Once calendared, the paper found its way to the trash.

- Choice #3 centered on reading important information needing attention but not requiring an immediate response. Examples included grant applications, letters from parents, and requests for information from the district office. After reading, and knowing quite well that these items could not be dealt a response in less than a minute I placed these leftovers in my "to do" file.

- Finally, choice #4, my personal favorite, was called the Slush File. When there was no other way to deal with a particular piece of paper, that is something could not be calendared, dealt with the next day, or thrown away, then I would turn to my Slush File. I would open up my lower left hand desk drawer and toss the item in there for future reference.

Items that fell into the Slush File included conference brochures and reports from outside agencies that I might need later but didn't want taking up file cabinet space. A large Slush File contributor was the mounds of grant applications the superintendent might someday want me to reconsider. After two or three months, my Slush File would be spilling over and I would spend an hour purging the drawer, most of which went directly into the trash. My Slush File saved me more times than I can remember. Digging in to find a specific conference brochure or locating an old parent letter thought inconsequential at the time but now needed by district legal counsel.

# 59.  80/20 RULE

The "Pareto Principle" or "80/20" rule has been around for a long time. Essentially it states that roughly 80 percent of the effects will come from 20 percent of the causes. In business this often translates to 80 percent of all results/clients/sales stem from a mere 20 percent of one's efforts/marketing/sales.

As a school administrator I quickly learned 80 percent of my time was taken up with employee discipline as a result of the bad behavior of 20 percent of my staff. This is a very dangerous trap. Although you must address the 20 percent fairly and swiftly, it is the other 80 percent that will ultimately determine your success as a leader.

Therefore, it is critical you make a decision as to where you will spend your time. Will you spend your time, a good 80 percent, going after a bad teacher, employee, or parent, or will you spend 80 percent on the initiatives and people who bring success to the organization? It's your choice; choose wisely!

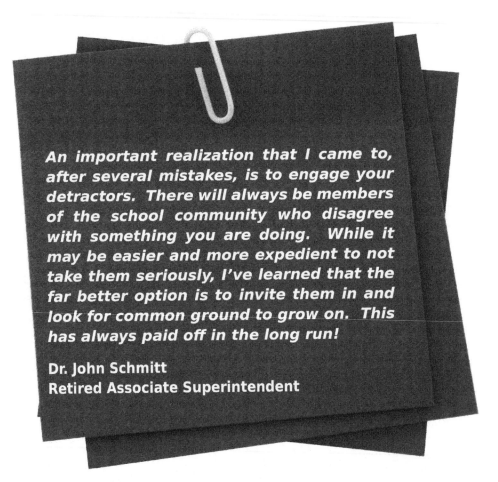

*An important realization that I came to, after several mistakes, is to engage your detractors. There will always be members of the school community who disagree with something you are doing. While it may be easier and more expedient to not take them seriously, I've learned that the far better option is to invite them in and look for common ground to grow on. This has always paid off in the long run!*

**Dr. John Schmitt**
**Retired Associate Superintendent**

## 60.   CROSS YOUR T'S AND DOT YOUR I'S

W e have all been told to document, document, and document. Throughout my career I have always been fairly good at documenting meetings, events, emails, etc. Not only have I always carried a spiral notebook, but still carry a paper yearly calendar around with me everywhere and have years of them kept in my archives. Ask me what I was doing on October 7, 2004 and I could probably tell you!

As a first year principal I truly learned the importance of documentation when one of my physical education teachers became enraged at a sixth grade male student who had jumped in front of the shopping cart full of PE equipment the teacher was pushing. Instead of asking the child to stop, the teacher rammed the student with the shopping cart with tremendous force. The student, in pain, yelled expletives at the teacher and the teacher reciprocated by getting in his face; he screamed and pointed at him in front of 200 other students.

Once I found out about the situation, I immediately contacted Human Resources and the teacher was placed on paid administrative leave. I immediately started documenting the incident by obtaining witness reports and took photos of the student's bruises, which ran from his ribs to his ankles on one side of his body.

I had heard rumors this teacher was known for being mean to kids and I was determined not to have him back on campus ever again. Due to the nature of the injuries, Child Protective Services was contacted and the case was turned over to the police for further investigation. I thought for sure this teacher would not only be barred from ever returning to my school, but the district as well. I found a file for the teacher that had been left by the previous principals and took a close look. In it, I found another incident that occurred where the teacher had injured a child. Apparently, the teacher would use a black felt tip pen to mark students' foreheads each time they ran a lap. However, this time he missed and the pen ran down the student's face and across his eye.

I also read about an incident that happened a few years earlier in which the teacher was alleged to have directed his eighth grade teacher assistant to take a sixth grader to the locker room alone. After everyone left the locker room, the teacher assistant attempted to intimidate the student and threatened to put his head in the toilet as a way to change the student's behavior during class.

I was shocked, and I thought that surely this would only strengthen the district's case, but it did not. The attorneys for the district found there was "not a pattern behavior." How could this be? Human Resources shared that of the prior incidences uncovered, only one official letter ever made it to the teacher's permanent employee file kept at the district. Therefore, a pattern of behavior could not be established and his behavior was not egregious enough to terminate him.

This story reinforces the need to properly document everything, even if it seems minor, because your actions TODAY can and often will affect the safety and well-being of students in the FUTURE. Had a previous principal crossed their T's and dotted their I's, this teacher would have been looking for a new profession rather than being transferred to a brand new middle school the following year.

## 61. WORK THE ROOM

As a leader you should use every opportunity to acknowledge employees or community members when attending large scale events. So often, I have observed principals or superintendents at these important occasions just sitting and chatting with a board member or close colleague and not using this important face-time time to their best leadership advantage. We know it's been a long day and sometimes it just feels good to sit down, but don't miss important opportunities to walk around the room to greet and converse with employees and community partners.

You are a very important person to them and when you take time before these events to work the room to greet people and thank them for attending, it's very significant. The visual of the leader connecting with people also speaks volumes. I once worked with a superintendent who was known throughout the district as a *curmudgeon*. In spite of his underground nickname, he was actually fairly good at keeping a lid on things, much like that of a store or restaurant manager, but he was far from what anyone would call a leader.

Month after month, he would arrive at special events and head directly to his assigned seat. He never took the time to talk with anyone or walk around the room. He would sit at one table throughout the entire event and barely converse with anyone sitting around him. Watching this same behavior year after year left me stunned. How did this man get this job? What did the Board see in him? The district was moving along okay, but nothing special. There was no excitement in the district, no overarching vision of where the district was headed; it was as if we were all working on our own. It was no wonder that our school district was known throughout the county for being one of mediocrity.

Leadership involves connecting with people, acknowledging accomplishments, sharing the vision, and establishing relationships. So no matter how tired you are, how shy you actually think you are, or how important that board member thinks he is, take time at these events to work the room and acknowledge those who support your school district.

## 62.  WHO'S THE BOSS?

As an educational leader it is essential that you establish friendships with your employees and maintain positive relationships with them. By establishing strong relationships in the workplace you can provide authentic leadership by knowing what motivates your employees.

These strong connections with staff make for loyal followers eager to maximize their skills, time and effort to realize district goals. However, as a leader you are the BOSS and you must be careful not to blur the lines between boss and friend in your honest attempt to establish positive working relationships.

It will be important for you to define the boundaries between yourself and your staff. No matter how close you want to get with your employees, you should make it clear that you don't want your relationship to be confused with that of a real "friendship."

Once you cross over that line from boss to friend, even with just one employee, you will create a perception of favoritism. You may not be aware of it, but other employees will be talking behind your back that you are letting your "friend" get away with more than them at work, giving them special favors or protecting them in difficult situations. And when layoffs or promotions are involved, those you have friended are often perceived as receiving special consideration.

I worked for an assistant superintendent who socialized with all of the employees, having drinks, and she was always the last one to leave the party. Everyone talked behind her back and no one respected her. She promoted her "best friends" to district positions and everyone talked behind their backs. It was a no-win situation for everyone involved.

While building relationships at work involves attending many of these social situations, and while it is important as a leader to socialize with everyone at work, be careful to keep your socializing in the office to a minimum.

You want to be respected as well as liked. You can maintain the respect of your employees by being clear with your goals. By setting up appropriate workplace boundaries in advance, you are demonstrating effective leadership to everyone.

Good leaders make decisions that can have an influence on someone's compensation, opportunity, and success. Keeping the lines clear between boss and employee prevents the perception that decisions are based on some kind of emotional bias and can circumvent conditions where lifelong enemies are created. Be a good leader; treat your employees as employees, and save your friendships for those who work outside your sphere of influence.

## 63. NEVER MAKE A DECISION STANDING UP

E ducational leaders make hundreds of decisions every day. Although most of them are made on the fly, it is important to recognize there are just some decisions you should not make standing up.

Sleep on the big decisions (firing, employee discipline, student concerns); you will be glad you did! Making a snap decision about something is probably one of the biggest makes a leader can make. With so many different decisions we must make every day, it's easy to understand our need for closure; thus the urgency to rush to quick decisions. I remember reading the only time things require an immediate response are if they involve the police, fire department or superintendent. Great advice!

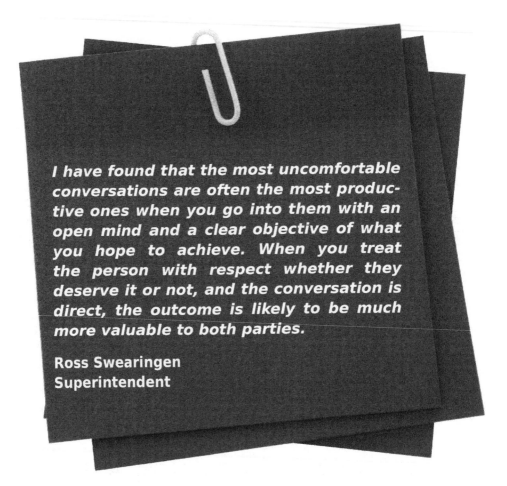

*I have found that the most uncomfortable conversations are often the most productive ones when you go into them with an open mind and a clear objective of what you hope to achieve. When you treat the person with respect whether they deserve it or not, and the conversation is direct, the outcome is likely to be much more valuable to both parties.*

**Ross Swearingen**
**Superintendent**

# 64.  4G SYNERGY

W orkplace demographics have shifted. Up to four generations (sometimes five) are now working together in organizations. Baby Boomers are often working longer and causing a
greater intergenerational mix.

Intergenerational teams provide an array of opportunities and
challenges. Embrace the uniqueness of each generation and do
not fall trap to stereotypes. Do not believe all "Millennials are
entitled and lazy," "Gen X'ers don't play well with team members," "Baby boomers are out of touch with technology," and
"Veterans do not want to work." Embrace the diversity and talents of your employees, colleagues and superiors and work to
create 4G Synergy! Some ways to support intergenerational synergy are:

## 1. Reverse Mentoring

Instead of having a veteran staff member mentor a newer
staff member, flip it and have a new staff member mentor
a veteran. This strategy is a great way for younger staff to
highlight their unique talents and share them with others.
For example, a veteran staff member could be mentored
in the use of technology.

## 2. Generational Defining Events

Build an understanding of each generation's viewpoints.
This can be conducted as a team builder. Have each team
member share a defining event that represents their generation (i.e. the assassination of JFK, Watergate, the
explosion of the Space Shuttle, the AIDS epidemic, and
the introduction of Facebook) and how the event shaped

them as a person and how it continues to affect them today.

### 3. Value Added

Focus on celebrating the unique talents of team members from all generations. Have each team member share a skill/strength that provides added value to the team.

## 65. STIFF UPPER LIP

We all know that it takes courage to make a good decision, even if it's unpopular. It's probably one of the hardest things we do as leaders.

Of course when we're making the best decisions for students, it's important to obtain as much information as possible within the organization. Try to seek out people's opinions relative to the decision you are about to make.

As a principal, one thing that shocked me upon entering the field of school administration was how so many decisions were actually made based on the best interests of adults, NOT children. Maybe I am an idealist, but I thought the main purpose of entering the field of education was to help guide young people to reach their full potential. However, I quickly observed practices that were counter to this. I saw teaching schedule requests being honored based upon a teacher's need to have first period prep to accommodate their commute or childcare needs. I saw our best teachers teaching honors or AP students rather than agreeing to use their teaching talents for students that needed them the most, all based on seniority. All of these decisions went against my values and beliefs as an educational leader.

Putting students first is not always the best political decision, as sad as that sounds, but it is always the right decision. Convincing our best teachers that our struggling students need them the most is no easy task. But if you can change the mindset of your staff and convince your teachers that it is an honor to be asked to teach the students who need them the most, because of their exceptional teaching skills, then you can begin to change the culture of your school and maybe, just maybe, students can come first.

As a superintendent, I recall one difficult decision involving our star basketball player. You will soon learn that sports decisions are the toughest ones to make since they tend to engender the most emotion from key stakeholders. This particular decision involved our celebrated basketball player, known for his winning game contributions. His mother asked me for help to move her child to another school district; she was upset with the basketball coach and didn't want her son near him. According to her, the coach had visited their home on many occasions in an attempt to persuade her son not to leave the team. She felt that his attempts bordered on harassment in that he was making her son feel guilty for deserting his team members.

The whole situation became very complicated and got worse as we headed into a big play-off season since everyone knew it was important that our star play every game. It was obvious most of the community was highly interested in this player since Friday night basketball was an important aspect of the community culture. For most, Friday night football or basketball was the main event in town.

The mother clearly wanted her child out of the district and wanted it "now." I looked my assistant superintendent square in the eye and tested the waters: Tell me, you know this kid, his family, the situation. Tell me what you think is best for this student? My assistant superintendent was a former athletic director and very connected to this athlete; I also trusted his judgment, as he was the type of person who was always there for students. Know this: when you reduce a decision right down to the very core, that is, what's best for the child, not what's best for the team, the school or the community, but what's best for the child, then the decision-making process becomes very easy. My assistant superintendent answered right away, stating he believed the best decision was for the student to transfer to another school district.

So there we had it; the decision made for this child was going to be easy, but not politically popular. As a result of permitting the student to leave our district, I received cold stares and jeers from people in the stands at games and was the target of several hate mail editorials in the newspaper. I knew, however, that I was being a good leader and that I did the right thing for the student and I could sleep easy at night. My decision was made in the best interest of the child and not for any other reason. Months later the student's mother called me on the phone and thanked me. She shared that her son was doing well in school and making good friends. And yes, we lost the championship.

## 66. STEP AWAY FROM THE COMPUTER

One of the most important things we can do as leaders is to be life-long learners. We live during a time when new information and knowledge is being exponentially created every second of every day. Staying at the top of our game requires us to stay current and also sends a strong message to our stakeholders that we value learning and expect it from those in the organization. It's important that we get off the computer and spend time actually reading professional journals, blogs, and magazines (in education as well as other disciplines) on a regular basis.

Engaging with people is also important. Attend conferences whenever possible and talk with as many people as possible. Some of my best learning has come from just asking others questions and listening to others. In other words, take some time to get up from your desk, step away from the computer, and get out there and experience and learn!

Formal education is also important. Over the last decade, doctoral degrees have become commonplace among educational leaders. To move up the ladder in some districts having a terminal degree is a requirement. In others, it is required just to be competitive against other applicants. Think ahead, do not wait until the job you want is open to realize you are under qualified; earn a terminal degree early on so you do not miss out on any opportunities.

## 67. THE SLIPPERY SLIDE OF "MY"

B e cautious when using the word MY in your conversations as a leader. Teachers make it quite clear that they do not want to be owned, and it fosters resentment if you refer to them as MY teachers when issuing directives. However, if you are defending them as a group or trying to gain extra resources from the district office or board of trustees then using the phrase MY teachers can work as a protective measure.

Board members also don't like being owned by the superintendent or other administrators and would rather be referred to as OUR board. Overall, avoid saying MY teachers, MY Board, MY parents, MY secretary, and try substituting OUR teachers, OUR board, OUR parents, and OUR school.

I once worked with a Chief Business Official who always referred to the budget and district funds as MY budget, or while shifting back and forth in his chair he would utter, "I can't spend MY money on that purchase." While he was a very talented money manager, people distrusted him because of his careless slip of the tongue.

The simple use of the wrong possessive pronoun can sometimes create unintended barriers in the workplace, often eroding effective team building.

# 68.   TALKING POINTS

As the leader of a district, department or school, random events of chaos can happen unexpectedly, often resulting in sheer panic or fear among staff or community. In times of crisis or confusion it is important to develop talking points to help people organize their thinking.

For example, when one of our most popular high school principals resigned unexpectedly due to a very confidential and personal matter, teachers, students and parents panicked and began to speculate on their own why he left his job. The gossip mill was in full force and ranged from the principal being held in lockup at the county jail, to his arrest for child pornography.

As a result we generated a list of talking points to explain the situation. Some of these included: (1) a statement that the principal left for personal reasons, (2) information that an interim principal had been appointed, (3) a promise that the school would continue to have effective leadership in his absence; and (4) encouragement to individuals to contact the superintendent with any questions or concerns. These talking points were then sent out to all board members and designated school staff to guide them when questioned about the situation.

By having talking points in advance, the district was able to protect the confidentially of the principal, put the brakes on the rumor mill, and provide staff the appropriate resources to speak intelligently when forced to respond to difficult questions.

It is important however, not to overuse this strategy throughout one's tour of leadership duty. The words talking points can often be misconstrued to mean "covering up the truth," which can leave a bad impression. To counteract that perception, always make sure your points are clear, truthful and shared by everyone. Remember, when a crisis or a confusing, complex initiative has dropped on your doorstep, take a moment to collect your thoughts, convene your leadership team and develop a list of key talking points that everyone can agree upon. Also, if the situation involves issues that could cause litigation, ensure that you run your talking points by legal counsel. Expert leadership involves thinking proactively when confronted with controversy or complex situations.

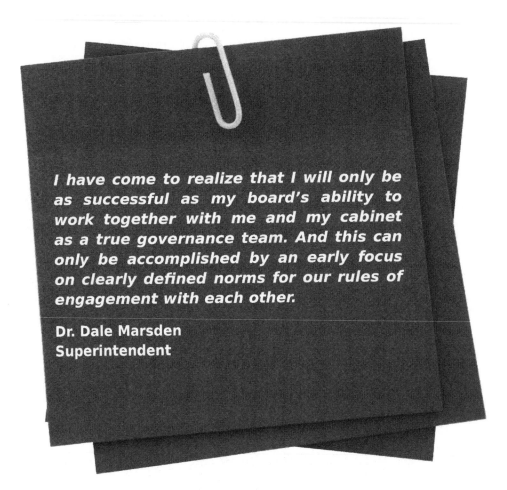

*I have come to realize that I will only be as successful as my board's ability to work together with me and my cabinet as a true governance team. And this can only be accomplished by an early focus on clearly defined norms for our rules of engagement with each other.*

**Dr. Dale Marsden**
**Superintendent**

## 69.  DEATH BY PAPERCUTS

It's not difficult to get surrounded by tons of paperwork or mounds of bounded reports in our business. After all, we just about invented paper, right? Why is it then that we continue to make copy after copy of things we deem important for our employees and stakeholders to hold in their hands at meetings, carry home for future reference, or store in that secret box under their desks?

As an evolving "green" educational leader, try your best to strive for brevity. Try it; see if you can condense an entire 30-page district report into a one-page executive summary. It's easier than one might think. Strive to communicate electronically for the good of the planet and to preserve your employees' sanity without going crazy by issuing too much paperwork. Be concise, be brief, and be succinct. Score points!

# 70.   DOWN AND FLIRTY

Most leaders have good sense about romance in the workplace but often don't know that flirting with a co-worker can also have negative consequences.

I worked with a high school principal who was on top of her game; in my opinion she was soon slated to move up to a senior leadership position, that of deputy superintendent. Over time I came to realize that one of the reasons she was perceived as being such a successful administrator was linked to how she chose to respond to men at work. Co-workers often gossiped that while she was a dynamo principal and leader, it often came with a wink, a slight nudge of her body on their shoulder, and just plain flirtatious behavior with everyone. She soon earned the name "Down and Flirty," losing a lot of her leadership credibly along the way.

On another occasion, I worked with a principal who couldn't keep his hands off the women employees or PTA moms. He was a real Don Juan in the community, but that persona didn't last long after our next superintendent was hired: a female. She found out about his flirtatious behavior and wouldn't stand for it. A year later he was fired.

Don't wink at your coworkers, keep your hands to yourself, and wear respectable clothing. Keep your party wear, especially if you are female, at home.

## 71. TO ERR IS HUMAN

S ounds like one giant platitude, right? We have been taught that those who gain success and happiness must be willing to learn from their mistakes.

It's true, you will make mistakes as a leader and you must learn from them. More importantly, however, if you don't take the time to reflect upon what you did wrong, you are bound to repeat the same mistake; thus lowering your chance to achieve your goals. My naivety as an assistant principal sometimes makes me cringe. I don't like to think about how uninformed I was. The good thing, however, was that many referred to me as a principal in training and were very forgiving of mistakes made. As long as I was willing to learn from my mistakes and not repeat them, all was good.

As a principal, however, making a mistake was a different story. People were not so forgiving. I remember one day, my first year on the job, a parent came knocking on my door. Poking his head inside the doorway he said, "I've got a free 15 foot palm tree outside, want it? I also have a palm digger and less than an hour before I have to return it. Where do you want it planted?" My parents had been complaining about the school's curb appeal and recently spent a full Saturday planting shrubs, installing flower boxes, and painting classroom doors. They were eager to make their school, a National Blue Ribbon nominee, presentable for the reviewers scheduled to arrive the following month.

"Sure," I exclaimed, "sounds exciting, let me show you a few spots that we might consider." Two hours later, a huge hole was dug outside the main office, just three feet from the main road. Five minutes after that the power went out for the whole city, and remained off for most of the afternoon and late into rush hour. It didn't take long for district officials to arrive at my school to ascertain the damage and assume their responsibility to the city. I knew I was in real trouble when I saw the superintendent climb out of a district car. He took me aside and said that while he considered me to be one of his best principals, he also said I could be somewhat of a "wild card" and chided that I needed to clean up my act if I was going to remain a principal. "What were you thinking," he scolded. "Didn't you think there were protocols for accepting a palm tree from a parent or that you needed to secure a facilities permit for this kind of thing?"

I know what I was thinking just then. I was thinking how lucky I was to have this man think I was one of his best principals. I was also thinking that I needed to think before making quick decisions. I knew if I waited for district approval to formally accept the palm tree that I would lose the tree for sure and my parents would be disappointed and an exciting opportunity would be lost.

But was that worth losing my job? Absolutely not. By facing my own embarrassment with some fairly serious mistakes, I was able to reflect upon my performance and become a stronger leader over time. Do not let failures cripple you. Keep in mind, throughout your journey as an educational leader, failures come with the territory. Administrators have a very rewarding, prestigious, and powerful role to play in education. With judicially applied power they are able to put their talents to work and make a difference for students.

Failures are often a byproduct of the job. Resiliency and the ability to examine and grow from one's mistakes is the most critical component for experiencing overall success on the job.

## 72. THE CRACKER JACK AWARD

In graduate school while earning my doctorate, the Dean would meet periodically with the entire class to acknowledge exceptional students. He called this event *The Cracker-Jack Award* for exceptional student success or extraordinary effort. The reward: a box of Cracker Jacks. I was one of the lucky ones to be honored. Upon first hearing my name called, I couldn't believe it. I raced up to the stage to receive my box of Cracker Jacks and knew instantly that I would duplicate this creative reward back at my school. The gratification and pride I received from receiving this small box of caramel corn was amazing.

Throughout my leadership tenure as a school principal, assistant superintendent and finally superintendent, I spent hundreds of dollars on these small but meaningful boxes of Cracker Jacks. I was mindful, however, not to award a box to someone without careful thought why they were receiving the award. As a result, these Cracker Jacks became a valuable commodity. I once overheard a principal on the way into our Management Council meeting whisper to her colleague, "I hope I win the Cracker Jack Award!" On another occasion I learned how important these little boxes had become when I awarded one to my secretary at an important administrative retreat for going above the call of duty to help an enraged parent. The next day I came to work and was shocked. On her desk was a large glass container, probably once used to preserve a flower arrangement. Proudly displayed in the overturned vessel, looking like a statue preserved for all eternity, sat her Cracker Jack Award. Acknowledge your people for their good work; make your tokens of appreciation become part of the culture. Go ahead; feel free to use the Cracker Jack Award at your school or district; it's a real winner!

# 73.   WEAR PATTERNS

W hen I was a junior high principal, the district office called and informed me they had received a grant to build a sidewalk from our junior high to the high school, since so many of our students were taking high school courses. "An architect will be visiting you on Monday," the district maintenance office reported. "Start thinking where you would like the sidewalk," he advised. "We also plan to build a few benches in the area." How exciting, I thought. I spent the weekend drafting what I ventured would be the perfect area for a sidewalk.

When the architect arrived on Monday, I asked him if he wanted to see my drawings. "No need, but thanks for trying," he replied. "Let's go out back and see where these kids walk naturally to get back and forth to the high school. Let's look for the wear patterns if we can find them." Sure enough, there they were, paths, worn out grass, trodden down dirt, all leading in a precise and orderly fashion to the high school. "That's where we'll build the sidewalk," the architect exclaimed.

This particular scenario served as a metaphor many times throughout my career, especially when coming into a new organization. Whenever I arrived at a new job or school district people would ask me, "So what are your goals?" I knew first, before charting out goals, that I needed to discover the wear patterns before making any changes. I needed to determine which wear patterns were still working and which ones were merely being used because they were convenient.

I shared this story many times when delivering my goals for the district. I described the wear patterns that I believed were still intact and should not be changed, such as instructional or assessment techniques, advisory boards, and award ceremonies. I also shared wear patterns that seemed to be growing over with grass and weeds and almost disappearing, such as teacher seniority for honor courses, lack of transparent communication, or weak budgeting protocols. By telling this story to everyone before addressing my goals, I was able to chart out goals that made sense for continuous improvement.

So take note, before coming into a new administrative assignment take time to get the lay of the land and discover the wear patterns within the district before making any decisions or charting out goals.

## 74.   ON-RAMPS TO SUCCESS

When working in the Central Valley, I travelled many country roads on my way to visit schools; we were in farm country. The Central Valley, known for its abundance of migrant workers, also had its proportionate share of English Language Learners. Their fate in our classrooms was not as encouraging as one would imagine. As a superintendent, I worked with my team to provide these students equal access to all available educational programs. This was not an easy task. Our team was well aware that English language learners often got trapped in the system as a result of poor assessments, poor instructional strategies or rigid master scheduling practices.

Travelling down these roads, day by day, I thought about the parallel of these students' lives with a country dirt road; getting trapped, not able to access the school's full programs due to their lack of English. They were stuck, in a sense, not having "freeway access" to what our regular English speaking students had, access to programs that helped them become career or college ready students. I imagined that our college bound students were travelling on a freeway, a freeway to opportunity. On the other hand, I imagined that second language students were constantly on a country road often having difficulty finding the on-ramp to the "freeway."

As a leader I knew it was critical to create "on-ramps" or program strategies, so to speak, that would give these special learners equal access to opportunity. While there is no one size fits all program for these students, gaining access for them is more about where they belong; providing them with good teachers, workable master schedules, effective materials, and meaningful assessments that would take them to the freeway of equal opportunity. As a leader, remember it's the on-ramps that matter for your special learners. Work hard to leverage your power and expertise to help all your students gain access to the freeway.

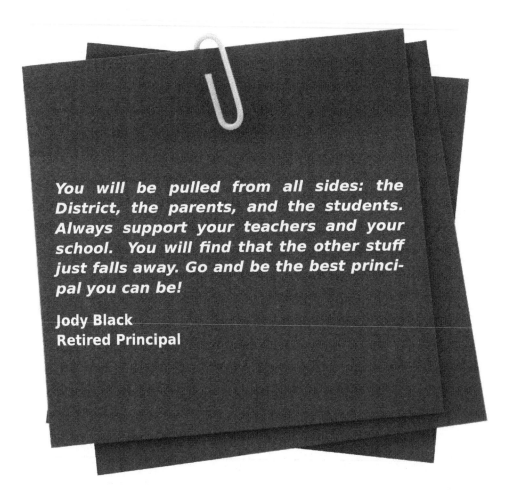

*You will be pulled from all sides: the District, the parents, and the students. Always support your teachers and your school. You will find that the other stuff just falls away. Go and be the best principal you can be!*

**Jody Black**
**Retired Principal**

## 75. T-SQUARE FOR EMPLOYEE UNIONS

Early in my career I created a mnemonic device called the "T-Square for Collaboration" that I often shared with union leadership. Each word began with a "T" and focused on key areas to help me remember how to maintain positive working relationships between bargaining units and administration.

This device may help you also when working with unions when you sense things are beginning to go south. Whenever I began to feel that the tone between leadership and union membership was not so positive, I would review my T-Square to see if I needed to shore up something in one of the "T" areas. I proudly present my T-Square©. Give it a try!

### 1. Trust
Develop trust by telling the truth and following through with promises.

### 2. Transparency
Share all information regarding budget, policies, and new programs in an honest and open fashion.

### 3. Teamwork
Work with employee organizations arm-in-arm to solve problems that affect the school, union members, and most of all our students.

### 4. Training
Provide and attend trainings (Speed of Trust, Interest Based Bargaining) to enable positive relationship building and problem solving.

---

Excerpts from *Rules of the Game: How to Win a Job in Educational Leadership*
Delmar Publishing, 2012

# 76.  SKELETONS IN YOUR CLOSET

**B**osses do not like surprises of any nature. If an incident at work or in your personal life occurs that could potentially spill over into the community, notify your district office or immediate supervisor immediately; they need to hear about it from you first. Do this no matter how embarrassing personally, since things can go from bad to worse real fast.

During my superintendency, my high school principal was making critical decisions at his school that were not always appreciated by everyone in the community. As a result of the repercussions, the local media began to take center stage. It seemed as if every day one could pick up the newspaper and learn something new about our school district.

Just when I thought things were beginning to calm down, one article reported that the vice principal of the school was the principal's brother-in-law. Since they had different last names no one knew they were related. This was startling news to most of us. Fortunately, these two were hired before I became the new superintendent, but nevertheless, I had to address the problem.

Two days later, things got worse. The newspaper disclosed that the brother-in-law had once been employed as an attorney. We were still recovering from the brother-in-law news when we learned these new details. An attorney, now vice principal, that's strange. Before anyone could get these two on the phone, a teacher came running down the hall, eager to share that she had read on the internet that the brother-in-law's license to practice law had been suspended. According to the internet report, he had become involved in some issues with a former client before becoming a vice principal. Our vice principal, then brother-in-law, and now suspended attorney, was working in our school district. Granted, this information did not play well in the media and as a result the Board of Education and community at large all wanted action; mainly someone fired!

Had we known these undisclosed details in advance, we may have been able to mitigate the fallout. When leaders know the scoop, they can get ahead of the game by sharing honest and open information with the media. If not, the media will draw their own conclusions or dig even deeper for more dirt.

## 77.   FAVORITE SON

As a first year administrator, I found myself getting frustrated as I was given more and more responsibilities because of my colleague's incompetence. I kept my discontent private, but I began to wonder how the heck my boss did not see what was going on. He was always so nice and complimentary of my colleague. Was he blind? This went on for months.

Finally, out of pure frustration, I said something. As we talked in his office and he listened to my concerns, he chuckled and replied, "Of course, I know that he is not doing what he is supposed to, but I cannot let anyone think I have favorites. I have to pretend I like everyone equally in public. I address performance issues in private."

Lesson learned: the appearance (yes, appearance-it does not even have to be real) of favoritism can be devastating to staff morale and your career.

This advice can also apply to nominating staff for awards. I made the biggest mistake of my career as a school principal after nominating a teacher for "Educator of the Year" with our Foundation. I was unaware that many colleagues disliked her and upon learning of her selection, the teachers sent a representative to my office to ask, "What are we, chopped liver?" This mistake took me almost a year to gain back my credibly with teachers.

While seemingly a small thing on the surface, having favorites as a leader can have huge repercussions. Don't go there!

## 78. BEHIND CLOSED DOORS

P art of the main job of becoming an effective leader is knowing that you must address employee problems and performance issues as soon as they occur. And that usually means in
private, behind closed doors.

I once worked for a horrible boss. During management meetings he would publically call out principals for doing something
he thought they shouldn't. If you happened to disagree with this
man in an open forum, all bets were off. He'd give it to you right
in the open and then not speak to you for a month. Not only was
it humiliating for the person taking his wrath, but we all felt
sorry that we were working for such a top down, disrespectful
person.

I doubt there are too many leaders like him still standing.
But in the interest of saving time, sometimes we get caught up
addressing an employee on their turf, in the cafeteria, their
classroom, or in the teacher's room. If you must share performance information or worse yet, termination proceedings, make
sure you deliver this information in a private office behind closed
doors.

# 79.   OUTSOURCING

As an educational leader, you likely moved up the ranks and are accustomed to being in the trenches. In the trenches you learn to fend for yourself. If something needed to get done, you likely just did it yourself. As a leader, the higher you advance up the career ladder, the more important it becomes to break yourself of this counterproductive habit. If you continue to take on everything yourself, people will soon begin to call you a "micromanager," or worse yet, think that you don't trust your staff. Both comments are derogatory and not something you want to have circulating around.

Letting go and delegating can be a difficult task but is necessary if you want to be a successful leader. Outsource all you can. Anything that can be done by someone else should. There is enough work that can only be done by you to keep you plenty busy.

Great leaders have a keen understanding of their role and priorities by promoting leadership in others and building a team of people (staff, teachers, and parents) to contribute to the effective running of the organization.

1. First, evaluate if a task MUST it be done by you or if it is something that can be outsourced? If it is not absolutely necessary for you to complete the task personally, decide who is best qualified on your team to carry out the task. Aligning tasks with people's strengths is the key and it should ease your anxiety of handing it over in the first place.

2. Once you have decided who is best for the job, set up project timelines and a follow-up strategy. This is a critical step for effective delegation. Delegation without follow-up will likely fail and you will find yourself staying up until 2 a.m. completing a task that is now due and remains incomplete.

3. Lastly, celebrate the great work of your team and show them your appreciation. Positive reinforcement will go a long way the next time you need to outsource.

## 80.   TAKEN FOR A RIDE

As a new superintendent I met with more than 60 parents each month who served on our District Parent Advisory Council. This group was intent on sharing what they wanted improved in the district. This two-way communication opportunity also afforded me the chance to invite their suggestions on how they could become part of the solution to problems. Issues raised included a lack of textbooks, a delayed stadium opening, benchmark assessments, inconsistency of the dress code at certain schools, cussing coaches and the teaching of cursive handwriting.

One problem area arose loud and clear above the others: student transportation. A concerned parent worried that our buses were dangerous and feared that her child was not safe. Another reported our buses were too crowded, while another revealed her child must ride the bus for more than an hour. Still another implied all the kids fight, the bus drivers have no control, and too many students were being forced to sit on the bus floor due to extreme overcrowding.

Finally, one parent suggested that the superintendent [that's me] might want to talk in person to some actual kids who ride the buses. "You'll get the straight facts from them," she advised. I accepted her challenge, taking it one step further. I would ride one of these buses — a 60-minute, 45-mile trip from our east campus on a bus packed with high school students heading home. This bus route was one of the more "dangerous" ones cited by parents.

I climbed on the recommended bus and immediately began to assess the situation. Yes, these parents were correct, the kids were big and the bus was crowded, but only six students sat three to a seat and no one was sitting on the floor. The students didn't know why the superintendent was riding their bus (nor did they appear to care), but they were infinitely curious as to why I was writing in a notepad. During my interviews with several riders, students were thrilled to report that 6 a.m. is much too early to catch a bus and confided the real reason no one on their bus ever gets into a fight was because, as one put it, "We all like one another." Those sitting three to a seat confessed they chose to sit with their friends, and everyone spoke highly about the bus driver. One thing, however, they all wanted to know was if I could use my clout as the superintendent to have a restroom and drinking fountain installed on the bus!

At our next parent advisory meeting, I was able to inform everyone that our buses were safe. "Yes," I confided, "the bus ride wasn't very comfortable due to the heat and dust coming in through the opened windows, but it was safe." If you want to become familiar with what your students experience, ride a school bus with them. If you want to demonstrate to parent stakeholders that you really care about what they think and care about their children follow up on one of their challenges.

---

Excerpts from "Superintendent Gets Taken for a Ride"
*The School Administrator,* February 2009

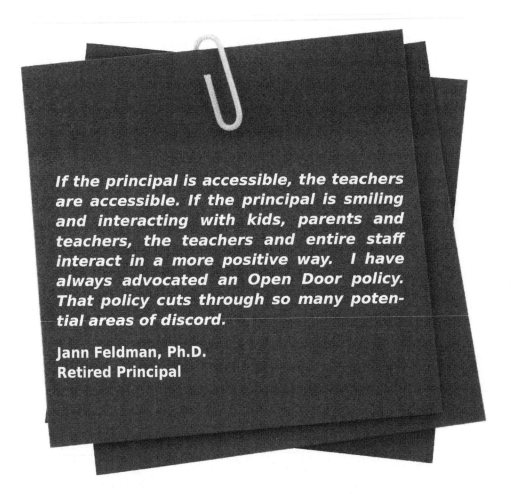

*If the principal is accessible, the teachers are accessible. If the principal is smiling and interacting with kids, parents and teachers, the teachers and entire staff interact in a more positive way. I have always advocated an Open Door policy. That policy cuts through so many potential areas of discord.*

**Jann Feldman, Ph.D.**
**Retired Principal**

# 81. SAVING FACE

You have read this advice a hundred times already. But 'fess up... you've been guilty of sending an email you regret, haven't you? Perhaps you've been lucky and not written an email containing condemning information, but what about the one sent with a glaring typo? Or possibly you've been one of the lucky email recipients?

I once received an email from my boss (meant for another colleague) that commented on a person I wanted to hire as my assistant principal. His response was that the person sounded good, but the only downfall was that this person was my "friend." This was quickly followed by several frantic attempts at "recalling" the message. With all the mobile devices most people operate from, the email "recall" feature is essentially useless.

As a leader I made two colossal email errors in my career. One blunder occurred in my role as assistant superintendent after sending an email to our junior high school principal. In frustration, the email described how sick and tired I was of having to respond to a certain teacher's complaints about the new math textbook adoption. I requested that the principal get this teacher under control. Of course you know the rest. "This teacher" was mistakenly copied on the email. The second gaffe involved an email appeal sent to over 1500 district employees requesting they make an effort to support our newly developed *Pubic* Relations Plan. It seemed as if everyone in the district was reading their email at once, as an onslaught of teachers and secretaries caught the mistake and let me know immediately. Three excellent rules to keep you out of email trouble include:

1. Never put anything in an email message that you would not want made public.

2. Write your email narrative in the body of the message first. After proofreading and reflecting upon your message, then type the recipients' email name in the address window last.

3. When sending out a large-scale district email, secure 2-3 top notch editors to proofread your message before pressing "SEND."

## 82. THESE WHEELS ARE MADE FOR DRIVING

Long commutes are tough! It's one thing to say you'll apply for jobs within a 40 mile commute and another to get the job and actually drive it. Before you settle into a long relationship with a school district, be realistic and ask yourself, "Can I drive a lengthy commute every day?" The drive may look easy on paper, but may be another story altogether when the road map turns into freeway.

I loved my job in Los Angeles County, but endured a long commute from Orange County for a total of two hours each day on the road. When it rained or an accident occurred on the freeway, my commute time could double. Relocating was not an option as my son was in high school and my husband was commuting in the other direction. So I chose to endure a long commute. Honestly, it was hard on my family, in addition to being physically exhausting and ravaging my Toyota with over 120,000 miles.

As an educational leader, your time will be very valuable and you need to manage it effectively. So, weigh the pros and cons about commuting before you apply for or accept a job far from home. Don't convince yourself that you'll only take the job for one year. That approach to problem solving seldom works. Once settled into a new job, most people establish close ties to their district and abandon all thoughts of leaving. A one year stint doesn't play well on a resume either.

# 83.   THE DATING GAME

Don't think for one moment as a school leader you can date an employee without first making some serious inroads on key district stakeholders.

For example, one of our assistant superintendents, recently divorced, was having a personal relationship with a district office staff member. It seemed that everyone was aware of this relationship but me, the superintendent. Had I known that he was dating the office clerk, I could have prevented some heartache and ultimate career damage for him. He was unaware the board had recently been involved with a high profile sexual harassment case that had caused them extreme anxiety and public scrutiny.

The district did not have a stated policy on employee relationships in the workplace, so when the board learned of the relationship, which they now referred to as his affair or indiscretion, they wanted him fired. The board was still struggling from the prior sexual harassment case. Had I known this information in advance, I could have shared their relationship with the board and recommended suggestions for how to proceed. The board probably would have agreed to openly acknowledge the relationship, given that the assistant superintendent was not the clerk's direct supervisor and was also a divorcee.

Having an affair with an employee, however, or for that matter with anyone if you are married, is off limits if you want to maintain your integrity as a leader in a school district. Words to the wise leader: avoid dating coworkers unless district protocols exist and never, ever engage in an extramarital affair. It could not only end your marriage but your career as well.

# 84.   NEVER LET 'EM SEE YOU SWEAT

It's one thing to let your employees or coworkers see you cry at work, but it's a completely different matter if people at work observe you getting nervous or losing your cool.

While crying often denotes weakness in a leader, letting folks see you sweat in tense situations "cries" out that there's a phony amongst us. It's very important from a leadership standpoint that people think you are really comfortable with what you're doing and believe that you know your role. If people perceive that you are rattled or panicked during a tense situation, they lose confidence in your ability to lead and start to question how you got the job in the first place.

Remember, in a crisis situation, keep cool under fire, or if you happen to find yourself in a circumstance where you don't feel very confident, at least be aware of this fact. Once you recognize your lack of self-assuredness, try to fake it. Act like you know what you're doing; go through all the motions and try to hide your insecurity. Rules of the leadership game: don't ever, ever let 'em see you sweat.

# 85.   BEHIND THE SCENES

A few years after the initial standards movement, I took over a high socio-economic school that was underperforming. It was clear from my initial observations that the majority of teachers' classrooms did not reflect standards based instruction. I could have easily created a list of what I wanted to see and proceeded to mandate it.

Instead, at my next leadership meeting, I created a brainstorming activity to generate ideas about what they thought a standards-based classroom should look like. Everyone recorded their ideas on Post-it Notes. Of course, to ensure a few keys items made the list, I participated as well. We then sorted everyone's ideas by major themes and before long everyone had developed a comprehensive list including my input, now so intertwined with the team's responses, no one knew who contributed which idea. At our next staff meeting our leadership team proudly presented "their" ideas about what they believed a standards-based classroom should looked like.

A quote by Lao Tzu expresses this idea best, "A leader is best when people barely know he exists, when his work is done, his aim fulfilled, they will say, we did it ourselves."

## 86.   CRYSTAL CLEAR

My boss, who never missed a day of work, planned to be absent from work for back surgery for a week. As his right hand woman, I thought for sure that I would be named "acting" principal without hesitation. Much to my surprise, he designated one of the other assistant principals, who was the least effective member of our team, to fill the role. I was shocked, a bit offended, and I thought it was a sign he did not trust me. While feeling rejected, I kept my cool and did not say a word.

Years later I mentioned the situation to my former boss and with a chuckle he replied, "Are you kidding? If I didn't make him acting principal, he probably would have used the opportunity to take the entire week off himself."

Remember, when things don't go as expected or when things don't appear as you think they should, don't overreact. Things are not always what they appear. Take time to reflect upon the issues before jumping to conclusions and don't assume the worst.

*Before you draw the line in the sand make sure you know who owns the beach.*

**Lloyd Wamhof**
**Advocate, Association of California School Administrators**
**Retired Superintendent**

# 87.  JUST SAY "HELLO"

S uch as a simple thing, one word is all it takes: *hello*. One thing you learn about building teams is the importance of balance between "task" and "relationship."

I tend to be very "task" oriented, especially early in my career. As a first year assistant principal, tasked with many of the major school responsibilities, I could be seen rushing from meeting to meeting, classroom to classroom. I was also just starting to believe that I was a real leader and not an imposter. Better known as the imposter syndrome, this metaphor describes when people believe they are a fraud and do not deserve the success they are experiencing.

These two inclinations proved detrimental to me as I attempted to find my groove and confidence as a leader. My focus on task and my sense of being an imposter often kept me from making eye to eye contact with my staff. I rushed around campus, often out of necessity, but mainly to prove I was a busy, important administrator.

All that came crashing down one day when my boss called me to his office and shared a letter written by one of the respected and well-liked veteran teachers on campus. In the letter she described a time when I was in the teacher's lounge placing notices in everyone's mailbox. Apparently, I was so focused on "task" and the feeling of being an imposter, I did not even bother to stop and say hello. The fact I had failed to say just one simple word, hello, prompted this teacher to sit down and write a lengthy letter.

It was a very valuable lesson and I was able to learn early on how important relationship building and acknowledging people are. So to all who are reading this book: hello.

## 88.  FUN AND GAMES

As an educational leader, having fun is necessary to keep your sanity. The daily pressures of meeting the needs of multiple stakeholders can be overwhelming. As an administrator I always looked for ways to have a little fun while at work. Moreover, schools are fun places to work and our clients, the students, are always enjoyable.

One Friday night I was assigned to attend the school play instead of the varsity football game taking place on campus at the same time. About a week in advance I created an elaborate scheme to impersonate our school's mascot at the game. The only people aware of my plan were my secretary and the drama teacher. During the play's intermission, I slipped into a classroom and my secretary met me with the mascot costume. After becoming the Panther, she led me to the football field. Once there, I danced with the cheerleaders, worked the crowd and pestered all the other school administrators on the sidelines by trying to get them to dance with me. Thinking it was a student inside the costume they all graciously declined. Being persistent, I kept returning over and over again. It was clear their patience was wearing thin.

Once I sensed they were just at the breaking point I gave up and revealed it was me by talking loudly from inside the costume. They knew instantly that I was the Panther. Every pestered person broke out in laughter and seemed to enjoy the prank. That night everyone had fun and to this day we still reminisce and laugh about this.

## 89.  NO GOOD DEED GOES UNPUNISHED

In education you can barely go through a week or two without recognition of some sort; National Teacher Appreciation Day, Music in our Schools Month, National School Counselor's Week, National Parent Teacher Association Founders Day, Administrative Professionals Day, Classified School Employee Week and the list goes on and on. In California, an entire web page is dedicated to a calendar of these special recognitions. In fact, the month of May boasts 27 entries alone!

As a first year Principal I did my best to stay on top of these special dates. A popular Mexican restaurant was offering free burritos for Teacher Appreciation Week. I quickly called and was able to order enough burritos for my entire teaching staff. I was excited to honor these teachers; they were the best!

The day came and I hopped in my car and raced 20 miles to pick up the burritos and return to school in time for lunch. I am still shocked I did not get a speeding ticket that day. When I arrived back on campus, I hurried down to the first lunch room on one side of the campus and delivered half of the burritos to a very appreciative group of teachers and proceeded to the second lunch room as quickly as possible.

Out of breath, carrying an armful of the remaining burritos, I walked into the second lunch room on the opposite side of campus and was greeted with pure hostility. One teacher immediately looked at the clock and asked if I was going to cover the five minutes of their lunch they lost while waiting for the food and another said if I did not have enough food for his classroom aide, he was not going to eat at all.

I was speechless and crushed. No good deed goes unpunished! As administrators we must be prepared for the unexpected harshness that some staff can deliver in times of stress, even though they probably didn't mean it.

Continue to do good deeds as often as possible. It's important to show you care in spite of any unintended consequences.

## 90. NEVER LET 'EM SEE YOU CRY

As we know, leaders are held to much higher standards in the workplace than other employees. In fact, women leaders are held to even higher standards when it comes to crying in the workplace. A retired Army sergeant once shared that women were once not permitted to join the military. "It's because of their tears," he answered. "Not only does crying hinder a woman's ability to perform, but the men are distracted by a woman's obvious distress and want to help. And for men, when it comes to crying in the military, a soldier can't go into battle with tears in his eyes. He might not see the enemy."

Whether you are male or female, employees who observe their leader crying report that they lose all respect for them. Tears signal the crier is weak, vulnerable, and unable to handle stress.

For example, as an assistant superintendent, I served on a hiring panel in which a candidate was interviewing for a high school principal position. The candidate was well known throughout the district for being an excellent administrator and the position just about had his name on it. Midway through the interview, the candidate divulged that his father had recently passed away and shared how he had developed courage as a result of the experience. In telling the story, he choked up and lowered his head for what seemed like an eternity. When he looked up, it was obvious he had been crying.

He gained his composure within a few seconds but it was too late. The district was looking for a strong leader and for them, crying in an interview was not acceptable. As a result, this talented applicant lost out on a position that could have easily been his.

So what is one to do if they feel the urge to cry at work? Here's a tip that has worked countless times whenever I felt the urge to tear up. Roll your eyes up into your head and look up toward the ceiling. You will immediately loose the urge to cry. Remember, cry at the movies, cry at home, but never, ever cry at work.

---

Excerpts from *The SeXX Factor: Breaking the Unwritten Codes that Sabotage Personal and Professional Lives,* New Horizon Press, 2003

## 91.   LET IT GO

I recall a slogan on a poster hung in a colleague's office that stated, *It doesn't take strength to hold a grudge, it takes strength to let go of one*. How true! Have you ever worked with someone that made you feel really angry and then you found yourself starting to ignore the person and perhaps not even speaking to them when passing in the hallway?

I shared a story earlier in this book about my assistant superintendent who openly stated his disdain for me as the superintendent. I was furious and had difficulty controlling my anger. For a few days I found myself ignoring him and getting angrier by the day. Most everyone in my leadership team was aware of the incident and knew that I was mad. My good sense told me that holding on to this anger was wasting my valuable energy and holding me up professionally. I also knew that I was working hard to build a culture of trust and respect, and building relationships in the organization. People were watching the example I set by my leadership, and it was critical for me to set the tone for forgiveness and progress rather than one of grudges and anger. It was important for me to decide to move on and let go.

I made the choice to clear up my head, which was filled with anger, and address the situation head on. I decided to approach my assistant superintendent and ask him to meet with me formally in a conference to discuss my concerns.

Before talking with him, I spent some time reflecting on why I thought he was so angry with me. I tried to put myself in his place and tried to understand why he behaved the way he did. In reflecting upon this situation I decided that it must have been difficult for him to accept an outsider like myself into the organization. After all he had been in this district since kindergarten and was targeted to serve as the next superintendent. That didn't happen for him and I'm guessing he felt embarrassed and hurt that someone else was selected over him. While I didn't have to agree with his actions of putting me down in public I at least tried to imagine where he was coming from. I knew he wasn't going to apologize or show any signs of remorse and that I needed to be the bigger person and put the incident behind us.

Our conference actually turned out rather positive. While he did not apologize, he explained that my style of leadership was not aligned with his and that he was having a difficult time working with someone who made so many changes so quickly. We discussed ways that we could communicate better and as a result the tone between us went from anger and hatred to one of neutrality. While I knew that it was important for me to forgive him in order to move on, I also knew that my act of forgiving didn't exempt him from his actions or change the facts. It merely means that I acknowledged him for being human and that we can all make mistakes.

As a leader, everyone is watching us. Effective leadership is all about building relationships and part of that involves forgiveness. True leaders know how costly bearing a grudge can be on an organization; it does not bode well for continued relationship building. While letting go may be extremely difficult, it is important to move on and remember to let all parties know what went wrong so that it is not repeated. Remember, great leaders don't tell you what to do, they show you how it's done. And holding a grudge is not part of that skill set. *Forgive, let it go and move on.*

## 92.   ALL WORK AND NO PLAY

E ducational leaders are known for having a short shelf life. Many who enter educational leadership positions leave within five years, much like teachers. The demands of the job are excessive and can be overwhelming.

One major reason for the attrition of school leaders is their lack of balance between work and play. The job of an educational leader can quickly become 24/7. I remember the nights when I would receive calls from the alarm company at 2 a.m. and with a coat over my pajamas drive to school to check for a break in. Yes, being an educational leader also means being a security officer at times. I would assert that in order to be a great leader you need to be a healthy one, both physically and mentally.

When I was hired into my first administrative position, the first thing I did was tie the laces on my tennis shoes and run. I knew instinctively that in order to have the stamina to perform the job effectively, I needed to be in great shape. Ten years later I still run. You must also find times to play. Play reduces stress, promotes creativity, and contributes to a general sense of well-being. Living a balanced life does not happen by chance. It must be made a priority. Here are some tips to help you accomplish a better work/life balance:

- Schedule 15-30 minutes a day for quiet reflection. Write your thoughts in a journal, read a book of your choosing, meditate, listen to music, etc.

- Exercise 3-5 days per week and eat right. Take a walk with your spouse, play some hoops with the kids, run a mile a day, etc. You cannot function at your best if you are not healthy.

- Divorce your cell phone. Give yourself a few hours every evening where you do not check your voice or email. Give the people you love your full attention. Email will always be there, time with your family and friends will not.

- Put family first. People respect and value leaders who put their family first. As the leader you need to model this behavior and lead by example.

- Take your vacation days. It is always tempting to skip taking your vacation days as you attempt to clear the never ending tasks off your to do list, but don't. Vacations give you a chance to step away from the grind, regroup, relax and ultimately will make you a more balanced leader.

# CONCLUSION

*by Dr. Tamerin Capellino*

In the game of educational leadership it really isn't about **WINNING** the game per se, but earning enough points on your leadership scorecard to **STAY** in the game. You see, *staying in the game* provides you with an opportunity to leave a lasting legacy; one that will endure for years, even decades to come. Too many lost points and you will be taken out of the game and much like the Stormers, you will not be around for another season.

Coming from a long line of educators, I learned this first hand. My grandpa, at the age of 34, became the principal of a K-12 Agricultural school in the small town of Tapiola, Michigan after serving as Superintendent of Brimley Schools for several years. John A. Doelle School was the first consolidated rural agricultural school in the state. The two-story red brick colonial revival schoolhouse still stands proudly, albeit run down and no longer in its glory, across from the hub of the town, a one-pump gas station and small market named Karvakko's owned by the same family for 80+ years (it is also still there after all these years).

The school opened in 1913 and served local kids until 1973, the same year my grandpa, James K. Allen, nicknamed "Jake" by his students, retired after an astonishing 25 years as Principal of the SAME school. This length of tenure is almost unheard of in today's educational world. During his 25 years of service, my grandpa experienced his share of gaining and losing points. To his testament, he gained far more than he ever lost and stayed in the game year after year. At the core of his leadership was a love for learning, a passion for kids, strong relationships, and community partnerships.

He earned points in a number of ways, sometimes with just the "small stuff," including giving students the keys to use the gym after school on many nights, selling his award winning pasties to fundraise for class trips, starting school carnivals, providing job recommendation letters or securing scholarships for students so they could attend college.

One former student shared with me, "[Mr. Allen] had a real knack for recognizing the particular strengths of his students. For instance, he steered a lot of his students toward careers on the Great Lakes, working on the ore boats, where the pay was good and the work was steady. In my case, he recognized that I had what he called 'a flair for writing'. He was correct, as I've been in the newspaper business for over 40 years."

His former students still laugh when telling others about the "Board of Education" (a paddle) he carried in his back pocket to be funny. In today's society this would have surely landed him on the front page of newspaper and a corresponding huge point loss, if not the loss of his job, but in the 50s and 60s, this earned you points, and A LOT of them!

He also earned points by initiating a hot lunch program, starting a Parent Teachers Association, and worked with community members to have the school named a historical site through the Michigan Historical Society. He also helped organize and finance the Tapiola Senior Citizens Club and even became a candidate for state representative to, in his own words, "do more [for schools] by being an area representative."

It was a rare occasion when he would lose points, and often through no fault of his own. During one of the yearly carnivals he helped spearhead, my aunt, his daughter was named Carnival Queen. It did not take long before a small group of folks started crying "favoritism." Of course, my grandpa had nothing to do with it; the Queen was selected by student voting, but nevertheless, he lost a point or two that day.

Being a leader was not always easy for my grandpa. One of his former students recalls, "The sad part was that he spent so many years being severely handicapped by his deteriorating spinal column. In his closing years, especially in the late 1960s, he had difficulty in even walking from the school to his house that was directly south of the school building. Pain was his constant companion. Despite this, he refused to give up--and he continued his teaching until the very end of the school's existence."

Even after the school closed, he never stopped teaching. After he retired, his leadership legacy continued every winter when he and my grandma would take the four day cross country train trip to beautiful Southern California to stay with me and my parents. My grandpa, although plagued with debilitating rheumatoid arthritis, made his way to the local elementary school every week to engage kids in Mental Math BINGO. I can still hear him saying, "What is 2 + 2, add 5, divide by 3, multiply by 4, add 3, divide by 5, divide by 3, add 4, what is the answer?" Back then this game was a novel concept and students would do about anything to win the neatly wrapped pieces of candy he had tucked inconspicuously in his front pockets. He became so popular he even made the local paper. Once I started school, I could not wait to bring his show on the road. I still remember the pride I felt "sharing" him with the rest of the students.

My grandpa had planted the early seeds in me without even knowing it; a love of and aptitude for mental math, a joy for lifelong learning and a drive to lead. Two of his three daughters became educators and five of his 13 grandkids followed in his footsteps as well. In his final act as a lifelong leader and teacher, my grandpa donated his body to the University of Michigan Medical School for use in medical research. After all his many years serving, he was still teaching others after his death. Now THAT's a legacy!

Only recently did I start to realize how far reaching his leadership legacy actually was, and still is. With the advent of Facebook, a John A. Doelle group sprouted up. Quickly, photos from the school were posted by former students across the country. My grandpa, as principal, was featured in many of them. This past January marked what would have been his 100th birthday and a picture of him was posted on Facebook in his honor. I was pleasantly surprised to see a slew of comments from former students quickly follow that further confirmed the far reaching leadership legacy he left behind.

As the granddaughter raised in the presence of such a rich "leadership legacy," it seemed only natural that I was drawn to teaching and leadership. After teaching for five years, I followed in my grandpa's footsteps by becoming an administrator in my early 30s. First, I served as a Student Advisor and quickly moved up the ranks, becoming a High School Assistant Principal and started a doctoral program a short nine months later and served as a Middle School Principal two years after that.

As I approach the 10-year anniversary of starting my doctoral program, I recall an exercise when we were asked to write a letter that described what we wanted our life to be like 10 years in the future. I was 31 years old at the time and my beautiful children were 14, 11, 7, and 5. It is always so interesting to look back and see how far you have come. Interestingly, most of the professional goals I set back then I achieved. However, I struggled with "balance" for many years (and still do to some extent). This is not an uncommon struggle by any means, but it changed my views on leadership and life.

I did my share of scoring and losing points as an educational leader (as you clearly learned in the stories we presented.) I felt like I was starting to leave elements of legacy, but I found my life was out of balance, and decided that my greatest joy and impact professionally came when I was helping to groom and prepare future school leaders. When I was offered a full-time faculty position teaching Educational Administration, I jumped at the opportunity. Not only is it important to lead in your professional life, it is equally as important to lead in your personal life. Making this move provided me more balance and time to accomplish both. Soon after, I was honored to be asked to develop a new doctoral program in Organizational Leadership. The program launched as a huge success and hundreds of leaders go through the program each year.

In my opinion, leadership comes in many forms: a quick text message to a friend who is struggling, a call to a family member you have not talked to in a while, a conversation with a former student who needs advice, a hug for a loved one, listening to a colleague, etc. Relationships are at the core of leadership; my grandpa taught me that. Another term often used to define leadership is the word "guidance." Guiding others to achieve their dreams, through authentic relationships, is at the core of what I try to do every day. I hope the leaders I help mentor, coach and train will be my legacy as they transform their organizations. The stories in this book are also a piece I hope to leave behind as well. Leaving a legacy does not happen by accident. As Kouzes and Posner state, "the legacy you leave is the life you lead." What will be your legacy? What are your stories? I encourage all of you to do some small act that supports your Legacy TODAY and if you feel like it, share with us what you did and your stories. We would love to hear all about it!

---

Kouzes, J. & Posner, B. (2006). *A Leader's Legacy.* San Francisco, CA: Jossey-Bass.

# ABOUT THE AUTHORS

### Dr. Marilou Ryder

D r. Marilou Ryder serves as an Associate Professor of Education in the EDD program for Organizational Leadership at Brandman University, part of the Chapman University System. Marilou holds a master's degree from Syracuse University and received her doctorate in Organizational Leadership from the University of La Verne in 1998.

As an educational leader, Dr. Ryder has been fortunate to participate in a wide range of experiences at both the university and school district level. Working in six school districts within two states, her experiences have included classroom teaching, leadership as a middle school principal, assistant superintendent of educational services, and district superintendent for both a unified and union high school district. Under her leadership, Calle Mayor Middle School in the Torrance Unified School District was recognized as a California Distinguished School and National Blue Ribbon School of Excellence. Her colleagues recognized her leadership by selecting her for the California Administrator of the Year Award and later was awarded the Johns Hopkins Outstanding Administrator.

Active in dialogue on educational policy issues, Dr. Ryder has worked with groups statewide to promote public education. Her leadership roles have included participation in educational women's mentoring groups and serving as a board member for various educational foundations. In 2007, Dr. Ryder was named "Top Ten Business Professional Women of the Year" for her involvement in local community affairs.

Dr. Ryder's scholarly interests range widely, from the history of women in leadership to that of mentoring teachers to become future school leaders. Her dissertation entitled, "The Impact of Male Gender Dissonance on Women's Potential Eligibility for Advancement to the Position of Superintendent" was later published as a popular book, entitled, *The SeXX Factor: Breaking the Unwritten Codes that Sabotage Personal and Professional Lives*, by New Horizon Press in 2003.

She recently authored *Rules of the Game: How to Win a Job in Educational Leadership*, a professional guide book that offers "Insider Tips" and "Trade Secrets" to help educational leaders reach their career goals. An accomplished presenter, Dr. Ryder speaks extensively throughout California, delivering a lively and engaging presentation entitled, *Boost Your Promotion Quotient*.

Throughout her career, Dr. Ryder has been an energetic and determined advocate for scholarly learning and practice and is deeply committed to raising the quality of education through innovation and sustainable change practices.

## Dr. Tamerin Capellino

D r. Tamerin Capellino serves as an Assistant Professor of Education and was instrumental in the design and successful launch of a new doctoral program in Organizational Leadership at Brandman University, part of the Chapman University System. During her tenure at Brandman she has also served in several key leadership roles including Chair of the Educational Administration program, Chair of the doctoral program in Organizational Leadership, and Instructional Designer. For this work, she was named School of Education Faculty Member of the Year in 2013. Tamerin also works as an adjunct for several other universities in their educational administration, teacher education programs, and doctoral programs. Tamerin holds a bachelor's, a master's degree, and a teaching credential from Cal State Fullerton, and received her doctorate in Organizational Leadership from the University of La Verne in 2008.

Dr. Capellino started her career in education in Santa Ana Unified as a 6-8th grade math and science teacher before landing a position in Corona-Norco Unified. During her time in Corona-Norco, Tamerin quickly moved up the ranks to student advisor of a middle school and a short nine months later to assistant principal of a comprehensive high school serving 3,200 students. Tamerin was recognized for Outstanding Support of Student Attendance by designing and implementing an innovative school-wide attendance program and her work also contributed to the school receiving a Riverside County Model of Excellence award. As a middle school principal in Lake Elsinore Unified, her school was awarded the 800+ Excellence Award by earning the highest point gain of all schools in the district (+56) and meeting all federal accountability requirements.

A genuine passion for leadership education has led Tamerin to serve as a mentor to hundreds of new and aspiring administrators through her work at the university and professional organizations. Tamerin was one of ACSA Region XIX's first mentors and was later trained as a master mentor trainer for Southern California. Currently she also serves as a board member of the region's Student/Associate Charter.

Dr. Capellino is active in scholarly pursuits and is known for her lively and informative presentation skills. She has presented at a variety of conferences for both small and large groups across the state, including: *Integrating Theory With Experiential Learning To Maximize Leadership Education In A Doctorate Of Organizational Leadership Program; Quick Collaboration: The Wiki Way; Technology Enriched Teaching: Trends In Blended Learning; 4G Synergy: Intergenerational Collaboration For Implementing The Common Core And How To Pass The School Leaders Licensure Assessment.* Her dissertation, entitled *The ISLLC Standards for School Leaders: A Comparison of Traditionally Certified Administrators and Administrators Certified Via Examination in California* was also published in *EdCal*, the Association of California School Administrators' (ACSA) weekly publication.